SAGE was founded in 1965 by Sara Miller McCune to support the dissemination of usable knowledge by publishing innovative and high-quality research and teaching content. Today, we publish over 900 journals, including those of more than 400 learned societies, more than 800 new books per year, and a growing range of library products including archives, data, case studies, reports, and video. SAGE remains majority-owned by our founder, and after Sara's lifetime will become owned by a charitable trust that secures our continued independence.

Los Angeles | London | New Delhi | Singapore | Washington DC | Melbourne

ADVANCE PRAISE

'*The 5Gs of Family Business* is a wonderfully rich overview of family businesses today and the many complex issues that they face. The book thoroughly describes the practices that business families need to embrace to achieve long-term family enterprise success and to continue to prosper for many generations'.

John A. Davis, *Senior Lecturer, Family Enterprise Executive Programs, MIT Sloan School of Management; Founder and Chairman, Cambridge Family Enterprise Group*

'Walter Vieira brings a fresh approach to a much discussed topic and uses real-life examples to illustrate that business families can and do take a larger view and bring a fresh perspective'.

Jamshyd N. Godrej, *Chairman and Managing Director, Godrej & Boyce Mfg Co Ltd*

'Did you know that about 70% of the top 500 companies listed on the Bombay Exchange are family controlled, and that two-thirds of India's GDP is in family-owned companies? In this readable and anecdotal book, Walter Vieira, an internationally known Indian management consultant, sets out stories woven from the many successes and failures he has seen in this type of company. These 5G lessons are not only for an Indian environment, but these are also internationally relevant, and will give any reader ideas for business success and sustainability'.

Lynn Haight, Non-executive Director and Past President, Institute of Management Consultants of Canada

'Walter's understanding of family businesses in India is both sublime and subtle, which makes his writing and assessment superb. Family business is one of the most complex topics in management, and particularly in governance. It has been a core contributor to the economic dynamo in India, as well as in many parts in Asia and China. Some have estimated that family businesses account for over 70% of the wealth, and thus the influence, in Asia. To appreciate businesses in Asia, one has to grasp the hidden drivers (including backseat drivers) behind family businesses. Family provides the first source of finance and labour, but family businesses also bring different challenges into any society, including potential nepotism, sibling rivalry, acrimonious fights for inheritance, the need for family legacy and control and, of course, the inertia for change. Family business has been a ballast for economic growth, either slowing down or propelling an economy forward with a massive undertone. This book is a valuable addition to any library and for those who truly want to understand the hidden mystery and might of India's businesses'.

Dr Gregg Li, Member of the Advisory Board, Center for Family Business, Chinese University of Hong Kong

'*The 5Gs of Family Business* is a pleasant guidebook for family business leaders aspiring for the continued prosperity and growth of their enterprise across generations. Experienced authors and consultants Mita Dixit and Walter Vieira effectively present their keen observations of successful family businesses, revealing the importance of five factors—genesis, growth, next-gen engagement, governance and giving back—to ensure long-term family and business success. Packed with interesting and insightful stories, and the nuggets of wisdom shared by prominent family business owners, this easy-to-read book is likely to inspire not only current and future leaders of family firms but also professionals serving these enterprises'.

PramoDITA Sharma, *Sanders Professor of Family Business, Grossman School of Business, University of Vermont, USA; Visiting Professor of Family Enterprise, Kellogg School of Management, USA*

'Family-run businesses constitute most businesses in India, as anywhere else. They are fascinating because of the mutual dependence of two ecosystems (family and business) that have inherently conflicting characteristics. No comprehensive picture is still clear on most aspects of a family business. As most of them enter the third and fourth generations, succession planning is one of the key issues confronting them. Walter Vieira's lucid and simple style in anecdotal prose will make this book interesting for founders as well as inheritors of family businesses and readers at large'.

Navdeep S. Sodhi, *International Consultant (Textiles and Clothing)*

The
5Gs
of Family
Business

The
5Gs
of Family
Business

Walter Vieira
Mita Dixit

Los Angeles | London | New Delhi
Singapore | Washington DC | Melbourne

First published in 2019 by

SAGE Publications India Pvt Ltd
B1/I-1 Mohan Cooperative Industrial Area
Mathura Road, New Delhi 110 044, India
www.sagepub.in

SAGE Publications Inc
2455 Teller Road
Thousand Oaks, California 91320, USA

SAGE Publications Ltd
1 Oliver's Yard, 55 City Road
London EC1Y 1SP, United Kingdom

SAGE Publications Asia-Pacific Pte Ltd
18 Cross Street #10-10/11/12
China Square Central
Singapore 048423

Published by Vivek Mehra for SAGE Publications India Pvt Ltd, typeset in 11/14.5 pts Sabon by Fidus Design Pvt Ltd, Chandigarh and printed at Chaman Enterprises, New Delhi.

Library of Congress Cataloging-in-Publication Data
Names: Vieira, Walter, author. | Dixit, Mita, author.
Title: The 5Gs of family business/Walter Vieira, President, Marketing Advisory Services Group, Mumbai, India, Mita Dixit, Head-Research and Consultancy, Center for Family Managed Business, SPJIMR, Mumbai.
Description: New Delhi, India; Thousand Oaks, California: SAGE Publications India, 2018. | Includes bibliographical references.
Identifiers: LCCN 2018041439| ISBN 9789352808656 (pbk) | ISBN 9789352808670 (web)
Subjects: LCSH: Family-owned business enterprises—Management.
Classification: LCC HD62.25 .V54 2018 | DDC 658.4/06—dc23
LC record available at https://lccn.loc.gov/2018041439

ISBN: 978-93-528-0865-6 (PB)

SAGE Team: Manisha Mathews, Shobana Paul, Ankit Verma and Rajinder Kaur

Dedicated to all the family businesses that we have both been consultants to over a cumulative period of 70 years.

We thank all these family businesses for the many lessons we have learnt, of what works and what does not—and when and where.

We have therefore been able to combine theory with practice, and write a book which is a distillate of accumulated wisdom.

We have kept it simple to create an interest in learning through reading and applying, so that family businesses will be better managed, and will make an even greater contribution to their enterprise and to the country.

Thank you for choosing a SAGE product!
If you have any comment, observation or feedback,
I would like to personally hear from you.

Please write to me at **contactceo@sagepub.in**

Vivek Mehra, Managing Director and CEO, SAGE India.

Bulk Sales

SAGE India offers special discounts
for purchase of books in bulk.
We also make available special imprints
and excerpts from our books on demand.

For orders and enquiries, write to us at

Marketing Department
SAGE Publications India Pvt Ltd
B1/I-1, Mohan Cooperative Industrial Area
Mathura Road, Post Bag 7
New Delhi 110044, India

E-mail us at **marketing@sagepub.in**

Subscribe to our mailing list
Write to **marketing@sagepub.in**

This book is also available as an e-book.

CONTENTS

RUNNING A FAMILY BUSINESS

Most of the world's businesses are family-owned businesses. Most family-owned businesses are small, many are medium in size and some are very large such as Samsung, Walmart, Ford Motors and Cargill.

Any small business firm started by an individual, in many cases, runs successfully for many years. However, as this person gets older, he or she needs to think about a successor—preferably another member of the family—may be the spouse or the son or daughter. Hopefully, one of these family members has an interest, passion or competence. Despite having agreed upon the successor, the initiator of the firm rarely leaves the successor alone. He or she has opinions on policies and strategies and may interfere too often with the successor. Eventually, either the leader or the chosen successor will give up.

The larger the family-owned firm, the more likely it will hire a professional manager. This might be done to avoid family quarrels about who should run the business or because the family might lack competent or interested members to run the firm. Hiring a professional manager with work experience, who has studied management, has earned the MBA degree, is competent and possesses strategic thinking could be a good answer.

But even then, the family has to develop controls over and rights of the professional outsider. The family usually appoints a board that works with the professional manager. The board spells out the rights of the professional manager and the rights of the board in cases of conflict. Some members of the family may want to work in the family-owned business and press for jobs for which they may lack qualifications. What is it that a professional manager can best do in this case, especially when he wants to hire the best people in order that the firm meets its objectives?

I am delighted that my good friend Walter Vieira has used his extensive experience and consulted with family-owned firms to write this book. Walter will address how a family-owned firm can survive from generation to generation in a world that is changing more rapidly than ever. There is an old belief that family-owned firms barely last for more than three generations. The firm starts up and grows from rags to riches. The second generation does its best to preserve the riches. The third generation starts losing direction or interest, and the firm goes from riches to rags. How to preserve and enhance the firm through today's volatile, uncertain, chaotic and aberrant times is a daunting challenge.

I have always loved Walter's business books. With real experience, anecdotes, frameworks and humour, they are always alive. They state the issues and bring worldly wisdom to enlighten and resolve the issues. Family members of a family-owned firm who read this book will benefit greatly from Walter's insights and wisdom.

Philip Kotler
S.C. Johnson Distinguished Professor of International Marketing,
Kellogg School of Management, Northwestern University,
Chicago, Illinois

Yet another book on family business? Is there not enough written on the subject, both in India and across the world?

Having worked with family businesses as advisors and garnered about 70 years of collective experience (Walter's 50 and Mita's 20), it was felt that there is still room for a *Primer* on how to make a family business run smoothly; how to make it grow in a volatile, uncertain, complex and ambiguous (VUCA) world; how to encourage the next generation to participate and grow faster; how to address conflict within the family; *and how to ensure joy, prosperity and contentment.*

Most owners of family businesses are innovators and entrepreneurs who have pursued an idea and chased a dream. They have a desire to update their knowledge and learn new skills. Yet, formal education through classroom learning or online courses is difficult because of a time-management challenge. They are too busy with their work. At times, it may be caused by the ailment of 'micromanagement'.

Our interaction with about a hundred owners revealed that most of them were tempted to read a book where theories, concepts, and dos and don'ts are presented in an appealing and easy-to-read manner. This is sought to be done by combining Walter's storytelling technique with Mita's insights into family-business-ownership dynamics through her interactions with business families as an adviser, researcher and mentor. The book leans on the extensive work done by established researchers and consultants in the field, such as John Ward, Peter Leach, John Davis, Pramodita Sharma, Kavil Ramachandran and others.

THE 5Gs OF FAMILY BUSINESS: WHAT DOES THE TITLE MEAN?

5G denotes a new *high speed* of the Internet in telecommunications. Family businesses need such speed today to survive and succeed in a VUCA world. Those who want to meander at a leisurely pace will be trampled and eliminated.

5Gs captures the essence of the *five core elements* needed to start, manage and perpetuate a family business successfully. The 5Gs are *Genesis, Growth, Gen-Next, Governance* and *Giving Back*. These are explained as a framework—through concepts and examples of real-life experiences—to create a ready reckoner for both young and old in a family business. We have tried to create a Global Positioning System which will keep *families in business* on the right path and in the right direction—now and in the future.

5Gs is not an academic book. It is a framework that provides tools and approaches for creating an outstanding and long-lasting structure of a family business. In the process, the book may be able to influence and increase the percentage of family businesses moving into the next generation, beyond the accepted figure of 33%,[1] as of now!

We hope that the readers will enjoy the book as much as we have enjoyed researching and writing it. We welcome experiences, anecdotes and stories from family businesses. Please write to waltervieira@gmail.com; mitadixit@gmail.com with your feedback. It would help us make the next edition more interesting.

PREFACE

---

[1]See https://www.forbes.com/sites/aileron/2013/07/31/the-facts-of-family-business/#6b17484e9884, accessed 3 September 2018.

ACKNOWLEDGEMENTS

Many thanks to

Professor Philip Kotler, the world's marketing guru
...for writing the Foreword.

Many thanks to

Mr Ajit Singh, Chairman, ACG Worldwide
Dr Habil Khorakiwala, Chairman, Wockhardt Group
Mr Harish Mehta, Chairman, Onward Technologies Limited
Mr Harsh Mariwala, Chairman, Marico Ltd
Dr Kamal Sharma, Vice Chairman, Lupin Limited
...for their contributions to the book, covering different aspects of the family business.

Many thanks to

Our family business clients and SPJIMR
...for enabling insights into the family business dynamics.

Many thanks to

Tharawat Magazine for permission to use material from Walter Vieira's articles in the magazine, and the *TOI*, *ET* and other publications from where many examples have been drawn.

And to

Manisha Mathews and the editorial team at SAGE, who helped to put this book together.

GENESIS
The Origin—Look Back to Look Forward

> 66 *All glory comes from the daring to begin.*
>
> Eugene Ware 99

GENESIS: THE FIRST G OF 5Gs

The world is now better connected than ever before, and we are an increasingly networked culture! Technology, globalization and digitalization are leading to a paradigm shift in our lives, the societies in which we live and the organizations in which we work. Our economic and business environments today are volatile, uncertain, complex and ambiguous (VUCA), as never before.

For a new-age entrepreneur, it is imperative to study the past dispassionately, understand its impact on the present and keep up with the pace of change. Otherwise, there is bound to be a failure, not because the business is outdated but because the entrepreneur is outdated.

An entrepreneur creates an enterprise. Genesis, the beginning of an enterprise, is akin to a seedling planted with a dream. It is nurtured by the passion and the courage of the entrepreneur, many times supported by family working along with. The culture of an enterprise is built by the values, ethos and entrepreneurial spirit of the founding generation. Over a period of time, the hunger for success and the level of perseverance required from successors change. If they make conscious efforts to regenerate the values and keep the spirit of entrepreneurship alive, only then business growth and continuity are ensured. When the business is a matter of pride, it becomes a legacy...across generations.

Indian business history is rich with success stories of entrepreneurs—the founders and succeeding generations. One such example is noteworthy.

It was 1894, and industrialization had taken roots in India under the British Raj. A fresher from a law school was sent to Zanzibar, Tanzania, by his company to argue a case for their client. Soon, Ardeshir, the lawyer, discovered that he had to lie or manipulate the truth to win the case. He refused to do so, and in spite of persuasion from the client and the company, he came back to India. His career in law was doomed even before it started.

Ardeshir Godrej firmly believed that India had to become self-reliant. After a flopped law career, he worked in a chemist's shop and then started manufacturing surgical instruments. The business did not do well. In 1897, with borrowed money, he started a lock-making business. Cheaper and good-quality locks were well received in the market. The business flourished. Safes were added as a new product line. In the first manufacturing plant, set on a large expanse of land at Vikhroli in Mumbai, the first product manufactured by Godrej company was not locks or safes but secure ballot boxes for independent India's first elections in 1952.[1]

The legacy continues. The 120-year-old Godrej group is one of India's most respected and diversified business conglomerates. Enterprise and ethics are the two pillars of the four-generation-old business empire. Sure, the structure of management may have changed with the times, but the innate culture of the Godrej family remains intact!

Family businesses in India have survived and thrived in spite of many challenges. Since industrialization in the 19th century till

[1]See https://www.thehindubusinessline.com/specials/godrej-group-enterprise-ethics-the-two-pillars-of-an-empire/article21689683.ece1, accessed 6 May 2018.

the era of globalization in the 21st century, the Indian economy has gone through several disruptions. Political upheavals have impacted businesses. Nuclear families, women in the workforce, increased opportunities for education and purchasing power of the great Indian middle class are the forces that have contributed significantly in changing the social fabric of India, not to forget the influence of Western culture through media and marketing. All along, enterprising family businesses have managed challenges by being adaptive and innovative, and at times through *jugaad*—constructive and cost-effective ways to solve problems.

Business models have changed and transformed over centuries. Families have evolved and generations have changed in their outlooks, perspectives and aspirations. But entrepreneurship, the foundation stone of family business, has remained intact. Whether a brick and mortar business or an IT start-up, family businesses portray some common traits across geographies, societies and industries. They are known for their innate sense of spotting opportunities, innovative solutions, long-term approaches, the quest for learning, a keen logic to evaluate risks and profit, and patriarchal leadership.

In the VUCA environment of global competition, survival and growth for family businesses depend on the agility and flexibility of organizations to respond to changes. Owner-leaders have to continuously develop new capabilities and competencies to steer their businesses ahead of the curve. In the era of digitalization and artificial intelligence, owner-families require to recalibrate their vision—change their conservative approach to a progressive perspective. A mindset change from short-term quick-fix solutions to long-term strategic planning is necessary for business founders and their successors to take the business to the next level of success.

Genesis is the first G of the 5G success framework for family business. Supported by other four Gs—growth, gen-next, governance and giving back—genesis remains the bedrock of core values, ethos and entrepreneurism in family business. It symbolizes learning from the past for progress in the future.

GENESIS: THE SOURCE CODE

Human beings are conditioned by genetics. There are those who suffer from diabetes, rheumatism or any other disorder that makes an individual and the family susceptible to such conditions, from generation to generation. This may soon change with research in the area of genetic modification and stem-cell therapy. However, at present, the challenge remains unsolved.

Family business resembles the genetic concept. The culture of family business evolves from values, ethos and core beliefs of the founder and the founding generation. It is not easily defined or documented in a text form. Culture is a dynamic aspect of the business. It is talked about, exemplified and lived. 'It's the way we do business here' is the theme, the part of the DNA of the family and, in turn, of the family business itself.

There is a term commonly used by computer programmers, *the source code*. Programmers specify actions to be performed by a computer, generally by writing the source code. It is a description of the software system inside our computers, which produces an executable program on the computer screens. The source code is as important to the users of computers as the values of the entrepreneur-founders in the success of the business. Values are the source codes embedded in the culture of the organization. When we deliberate on them, we find three source codes that create the success profile of family business: integrity, discipline and concern (IDC).

While thinking about astute family businesses such as Tata or Murugappa, Bajaj or Mahindra, and Wipro or Godrej, there is an immediate connect with the three source codes of these companies. They do honest business with integrity, they work hard with discipline and rules in place, and they show concern for customers, employees and the community. There are thousands of successful companies, small- and medium-sized enterprises besides large corporates, which have been founded on the firm ground of honesty and hard work. These values have to be aligned with the vision, goals and competence, all required to take the enterprise forward.

There are companies wherein the founders and promoters themselves have ignored all or some of the source codes of IDC. They have gone into a spin where they have lost their reputation and, most often, their kingdom. The diamond merchant Nirav Modi, Vijay Mallya of Kingfisher Airlines and Ramalinga Raju of Satyam Computers are some of the known examples of recent time.

Many years ago, Winston Churchill was reported to have remarked, 'Behind every great fortune is a great crime'. It would imply that in the foundation of every significantly successful business is a large layer of wrongdoing. It is not always true; yet ignoring this perception means turning a blind eye to the truth. It is commonplace for the succeeding generations to be corrupted by money and power, and compromise on IDC.

Popular press are filled with stories of scions of billionaire families involved in reckless demonstrations of their exuberance. A leading daily gave a listing of such scions involved in car accidents when driving their fancy cars recklessly. August Busch IV, heir to the Anheuser-Busch Brewery, was one of them, who had many skirmishes with the law and finally sold the family company for $51 billion and retreated from the public eye. Marco Muzzo, grandson of a Canadian property billionaire, was awarded 10 years in prison for crashing his jeep into a car in Ontario. Thor Batista, son of the Brazilian business magnate Elke Batista—once the seventh richest man in the world—and even Alice Walton, heiress to the Walton fortunes from Walmart—who is worth $40 billion—have been arrested multiple times for driving under the influence.

The Skol Beer company wound up operations after 150 years when the fourth generation Skol ran the company to the ground. He was more attached to his hobby of photography than running the business, while maintaining a lavish lifestyle. The heir to Samsung company, Jay Y. Lee, was jailed for bribing the former president of South Korea, Park Geun-hye. The president lost her position—and so did Lee—apart from bringing shame and ignominy to the Samsung brand name.

The German economist Max Weber estimated that only 13% of family companies reach the third generation and 3% reach the fourth. Examples of succeeding generations failing in the business clearly indicate that for success and perpetuity, values and ethics have to be deeply embedded in the culture of the family and the business. Then the business does not remain a means of livelihood or a mechanism to create wealth for the family, but it also enhances value for stakeholders and is responsible to the environment. Weak and compromised ethics and values are many a time the raison d'être for the failure of family businesses. That is why it is the cycle of life for companies as with human beings—though our attempt is always to lengthen the time period to the longest possible. A strong foundation of values is a part of the answer, apart from the relevance of the business to a changing environment in a VUCA world!

ENTREPRENEUR: THE BUZZWORD

The one who seeks opportunities for profit and by doing so creates new markets and fresh opportunities is an entrepreneur. It is the buzzword of the 21st century.

Being innovative and taking risks are the hallmarks of entrepreneurs, across the globe and throughout civilizations. Spirit of enterprise is a common thread that has tied humankind, from the Stone Age to the Age of Artificial Intelligence.

The word 'entrepreneur' appeared in the French dictionary in 1723 to describe a person who organizes and operates a business by taking financial risk. Over time, the meaning has got modified. Now, we have the *incubator* entrepreneur, the *internal* entrepreneur, the *freelance* entrepreneur, the *hobbyist-turned* entrepreneur and the *un-job* entrepreneur. The meaning of the word entrepreneur has been stretched to such an extent that one may wonder whether its usefulness remains or has got eroded (O'Connell 2014).

In the 21st century, the entrepreneurial ventures have taken a new shape and form as 'start-ups'. A favoured career choice, start-ups are fuelling the entrepreneurial spirit of the millennials. Jason Haber, a serial and social entrepreneur, explains in his book, *The Business of Good*, why today's millennial generation may just be the best entrepreneurial generation ever. Born between 1980 and 2000, the millennials have ignored or disregarded the life and career patterns so formally laid out by their senior generation. Patience is not in their DNA. They don't wait for taxis; they take Uber. They don't wait for emails; they text. They don't wait to work up the corporate ladder; they start their own business. Everything is about today, about this moment. Millennials do not want to wait to make a difference (Haber 2016).

ARE ENTREPRENEURS BORN OR MADE?

The debate goes on whether entrepreneurial characteristics are genetic, or whether entrepreneurship is a skill that can be learned. A group of researchers studied behavioural and molecular genetics of entrepreneurship by looking at a general pool of people, as well as identical and fraternal twins. They tested the number of businesses a person had started, the length of time someone was self-employed and other factors such as the desire to run a business. They found that the genetic tendency to become an entrepreneur is 37%–48%. The tendency to identify new business opportunities is in the genes of millennials. Also, the tendency to have personality traits such as extroversion and openness has a genetic component. It means that an individual's gene could affect his or her tendency to be an entrepreneur by influencing the type of the personality the individual develops (Heitzman 2015).

A research by PwC on family business succession showed that almost half of the entrepreneurs come from family-run businesses, highlighting that the spirit of entrepreneurship is still lying at the heart of many family businesses. Around 54% of respondents in the survey expressed their desire to set up their own entrepreneurial ventures.[2]

So the moot question is: Are entrepreneurs born or made? Are they a unique breed with a drive and need to succeed which most people do not possess, or can they be created through education, experience and guidance? Research has indicated that there may be people with certain genetic characteristics and personality traits who are more likely to succeed as entrepreneurs than others.

---

[2]The Family Business Sector in 2016: Success and Succession, https://www.pwc.com/gx/en/services/family-business/family-business-survey-2016/succession.html, accessed 6 June 2018.

In his 2010 book, *Born Entrepreneurs, Born Leaders*, Scott Shane, professor of entrepreneurial studies at Cleveland's Case Western Reserve University, suggested that genes don't just influence whether a person will start a business, they may even determine how much money a person will earn. In other words, some people are born to be alpha wolves, and the rest will work in the mailroom (*Entrepreneur* 2013).

Musings

Our world that we know today—of machines, aircrafts, automobiles, telephones, computers, the Internet and Sophia, a social humanoid robot—is a reflection of scientific enterprise of only last 300 years. The roots of entrepreneurship can be racked about 20,000 years ago. The first known trading between humans took place in New Guinea around 17,000 BCE, where locals would exchange obsidian (a volcanic glass prized for its use in hunting tools) for other needed goods such as tools, skins and food.

Entrepreneurship is truly a dynamic phenomenon, as old as human civilization!

Reflexion: Three Traits of Entrepreneurs

In the millennial generation, we will see the three factors—openness, conscientiousness and disagreeability (OCD)—being used more widely than they were used in the previous generations. The VUCA world encourages it, and the younger generation makes faster progress than was possible in the past.

Malcolm Gladwell (the author of several bestselling books such as *The Tipping Point* and *David and Goliath*) spoke at the World Business Forum in New York, where he said that successful entrepreneurs have three traits—OCD—which they combine. This combination does not happen often, but when it does, the combination produces people such as Ingvar Kamprad, the founder of IKEA, and Steve Jobs of Apple.

Gladwell says that the combination of openness and conscientiousness is as scarce as it is powerful. There is no dearth of people who are creative without being conscientious. And again, there are people who are conscientious (like accountants) but not creative. It is rare to have both these qualities in combination—to be someone with both an imagination to draw up some radical way of doing things and the relentless focus to make it happen.

Add to that the third factor, that is, one must be disagreeable. There are few people willing to take social risks, to do things others may disapprove of. It is not easy. Society frowns on disagreeableness. We are conditioned to seek the approval of those around us. Yet radical thought needs to challenge convention if one is going to make a difference to the community, to the nation and to the world.

Gladwell gives the example of Kamprad, who showed 'openness' with developing a new method of making furniture and was conscientious enough to expand his business relentlessly, but was also disagreeable to all his fellow Swedes when he decided to outsource the manufacturing of Ikea furniture to Poland, at the height of the Cold War. His compatriots called him a 'traitor'. He was disagreeable. He did not care! The result: founded in 1943 in Älmhult, Sweden, Kamprad's IKEA has become the world's largest furniture retailer with a global revenue exceeding 35 billion euros in 2016.

A similar case was reported in our home turf. Bindeshwar Pathak was an engineer in the Bihar state government who developed a new sanitation system which would be cheaper to construct and maintain, and would generate biogas to provide energy—a landmark development for India, a country where over 50% of the population does not have sanitation facilities. Pathak had openness and conscientiousness, but the government authorities were not impressed. They would not fund Pathak's invention the Sulabh Shauchalaya model (SS), which he had a plan to set up throughout India. So he quit the job and at a great risk started Sulabh International Social Service Organization in 1970, combining technical innovation with humanitarian principles.

Thirty years later, the SS toilets are found throughout the country, and Pathak has won many accolades and recognition internationally. He is a Padma Bhushan recipient from the Government of India and a UN consultant on sanitation, whose expertise is used today in developing countries of continents such as Africa, South America and Asia!

Pathak, like Kamprad, had demonstrated a rare combination of the three traits—OCD. Always the mark of the founders of the family business! Can this formula be transmitted from the entrepreneur-founder to his progeny?

A difficult question to answer—but one wishes that it was always possible.

And anyone born after 1980 has a fundamentally different approach to the world than everyone else, creating both challenges and opportunities between the generations.

Musings

Founders can be responsible for ruining their companies. On one side, there is a co-founder like Sergey Brin of Google, and on the other side is Michael S. Dell, the founder and CEO of Dell Technologies. Google became the most valuable company in the world, whereas Dell, once the largest computer systems provider in the world, ultimately lost its leadership due to poor decisions, lack of product innovation and legal woes.

Lazaridis and Jim Balsillie founded BlackBerry and pioneered the smartphone revolution. Lazaridis failed to prepare BlackBerry for competition from rivals and had to back out from the market and, therefore, lost the market.

Three apparent reasons for such performance of founders are as follows: lack of agility and vision to transform their companies when their markets change, lack of foresight and resistance to let go of their commanding position at the right time.

Source: *McIntyre, Hess and Weigley (2013)*

CONTRIBUTION OF FAMILY BUSINESS, WORLDWIDE

The global marketplace may have turned complex and competitive, but family businesses always have a place to sustain and grow. It is no exaggeration to say that family business is the foundation of all economic activities in the world. Nearly all businesses start with an individual, then the family, then a corporation and then reinvent themselves or die. Some sooner, some later or sometimes much later.

According to a study by the Boston Consulting Group, family business is defined on two elements: the family must own a significant share of the company and be able to influence important decisions, and there must be a transition or planning for transition to the next generation. Based on this definition, the finding of the study is that 33% of companies in America and 40% in France and Germany are family businesses with revenues of more than $1 billion a year. In Asia and Brazil, they are even more prevalent, as depicted in Figure 1.1 (*The Economist* 2012).

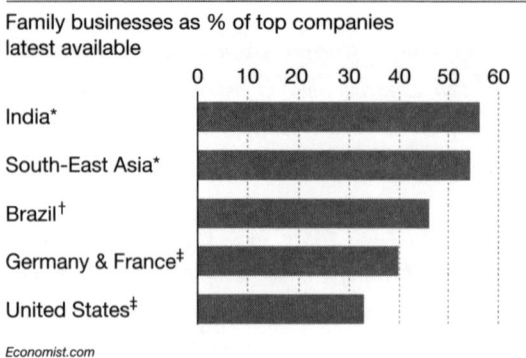

FIGURE 1.1 FAMILY MATTERS

Family businesses as % of top companies
latest available

Economist.com

Source: Boston Consulting Group
Notes: *Top 200 companies by revenue
†Companies with revenues over $500 m
‡Companies with revenue over $1bn

Across the world, the significance of family businesses as GDP contributors and wealth creators is undoubtedly high. One-third of the 1,000 largest companies in the world are controlled by families. Our research suggests that almost 70% of India's top 500 Bombay Stock Exchange listed companies (by market capitalization, 2009) are family controlled.

According to KPMG's report *Family Firm: The India Perspective, 2013*, family companies account for two-thirds of India's GDP and for 90% of the gross industrial output. About 27% of overall employment and 79% of organized private sector employment is generated by family businesses (Figure 1.2).

Statistics are derived from real cases and pieces of evidence of how wealthy the families can be. One such example is of Cargill. It is one of the oldest companies in the USA, still

FIGURE 1.2 FAMILY BUSINESS CONTRIBUTION (%) TO NATIONAL GDP

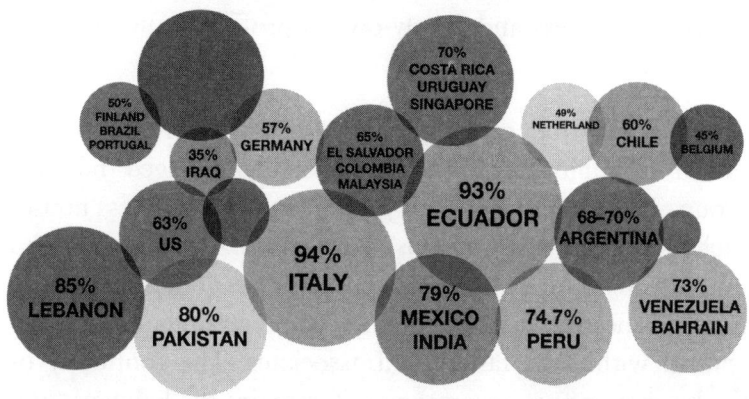

Source: Family Firm Institute, https://www.ffi.org/page/GlobalDataPoints

a family-owned and family-controlled company with a $108 billion revenue and an employee strength of over 155,000 in 70 countries. The company has created wealth for itself as a corporate, and also for their employees and stakeholders. Indeed, the owner-promoters do get their share of the pie, which explains how the family has 14 billionaire family members, more than any other family in the world, according to a Forbes report (Baermar 2015).

INDIA'S FAMILY BUSINESS: AN ENDURING HISTORY

Many times, a question is asked: Whether the Tata group is a family business?

Family businesses are omnipresent, yet have diverse connotations and inferences based on ownership, voting rights, strategic intent, size and type of families, etc. Two popular distinctions of Indian family business are family-owned-and-managed business and family-owned-professionally-managed business.

To answer the Tata group question, we nod in affirmation and call it a family-controlled-professionally-managed business group. The modern avatar of prominent large business houses such as the Birlas, Ambanis, Piramals, Bajaj, Munjals and Burmans has empowered non-family professionals to manage their businesses with a free hand while retaining ownership control within the family and associates. The continuity of the business across generations still remains the hallmark of a family business.

Early Times

India's business roots are as old as the Indus Valley Civilization of 2500 BC. It was one of the most progressive civilizations that the world has ever seen—business and trade existed at that time. The civilization came to an end for unknown reasons; yet the spirit of enterprise in India lived on. Several studies on Indian business history show that for centuries, India has occupied a dominant role in the world of commerce.

The origin of the family business concept in the world is not known in terms of place and time. In India, its genesis lies in the agrarian society structure, trading occupations and social culture of joint families. For centuries, families of siblings and extended families of their children—the cousins—lived together, worked in the same trade, shared expenses and distributed earnings. Joint families were the prime socio-economic characteristic of India for the simple division of labour, sharing livelihood, and prevalence of customs and traditions.

Over a period, a collective group of such families became communities with their own culture, and practices of doing the business and managing families. Practically all business activities were concentrated in the so-called trading communities. Bania, Marwari, Bhatia, Sindhi and Chettiar were some of the prominent communities stratified occupationally.

The concept of family businesses as trading communities, flourished under the Mogul reign (1526–1858 AD). During this period, India experienced unprecedented prosperity. Indian merchants controlled large sectors of trade in Central Asia, Southeast Asia and Iran. India's abundances attracted traders from Europe, and the seeds of the British Raj were sown with the East India Company (FICCI 1999). It is said that in the 16th century, the GDP of India was estimated at about 25.1% of the world economy, as compared to 7.45% in 2017.[3]

Industrialization began around the middle of the 1800s under the British rule. The turning point for Indian industry came during the First World War. Businesses of the British in India were impacted by the war, so some enterprising young traders grabbed the opportunity and ventured into manufacturing. Cotton textiles and yarn mills were the first start-ups. Entrepreneurs from several trading communities such as Parsi, Khoja, Bhatia and Jain became prominent industrialists (Das 1999).

During the 1930s and 1940s, pioneers such as Tata, Lala Shriram, Walchand Hirachand, Mafatlals, Kirloskars, T.V. Sundaram Iyengar, Birla, Podar and Bangur had established businesses in textiles, sugar, construction, agribusinesses,

---

[3]History of Indian Economy, http://cgijeddah.mkcl.org/WebFiles/History-of-Indian-Economy.pdf, accessed 6 June 2018.

aircraft, machines, electricals, etc. Industrial enterprises were more risky than trading businesses as the money requirement was large with longer gestation periods and slower returns. To spread the risk, the families setting up industrial undertakings enlisted the cooperation of close friends and relatives, and allotted them blocks of shares while making sure that the majority control and the management of the company remained with the promoting family. This way, a system of corporate management was born which was a strange combination of joint stock principle and family control (Tripathi 1999).

Along with the freedom movement, businesses grew. New industries, products and brands took birth. Silent movies and the music industry were developed during the early 1900s. India was not only fighting for freedom but had started taking baby steps of being self-reliant.

Post Independence

With Independence, a new era emerged in 1947. Numerous business communities and entrepreneurs prepared themselves for the challenges of building a new, independent nation in the years to come. Out of 127 large companies in India, 58 were under foreign or British management. Many popular brands such as Dalda, Air-India, Horlicks, Iodex, All India Radio, Rajshri Productions and Duckback raincoats were born in and around 1947. Several of them even today represent the enterprising spirit of India.

During the 1950s, the most prominent industrial firms on the concourse of Indian businesses were in the hands of just 18 Indian families and two British houses (Tripathi 1992). In the 1960s and 1970s, there were about 75 business families who had monopoly on core industries and products. They attracted attention of the government. To ensure that the concentration of economic power in operation of the economic system does not remain in the hands of a few rich, the Monopolies and Restrictive Trade Practices Act (MRTP Act) was passed in 1969.

The private sector firms had to operate in a restrictive, protected atmosphere, constrained by the licence-permit dispensation, known as the Licence Raj. Government policies obstructed external trades and the development of financial markets. In spite of constraints, family groups grew and kept dominating the Indian economy.

The building blocks of success during the post-Independence period for enterprising business houses were their ability to hire good people, treat them well, be focused and get the factories running as quickly as possible. Successful entrepreneurs such as Rama Prasad Goenka and Dhirubhai Ambani were cast in this mould (Sampath 2001). Some of the successful industrialists like Goenka had a sound family business base, and some such as Ambani emerged from a modest middle-class background to become a textile and petrochemical magnate.

This era also saw the emergence of new industrialists who took advantage of government policies as well as the stock market's equity cult. Between 1975 and 1990, India's domestic private sector was given greater room to manoeuvre the regulatory economy (Mukherji 2009). The Ruias, Mittals, Jindals, etc. came up because of the thrust in the sponge iron sector. Many technocrat entrepreneurs and business houses in pharma and cement such as Sun Pharma, Reddy's Laboratories, Nagarjuna Group and Raasi Cement emerged.

Musings

This is an interesting story of a third-generation Kirloskar going to Egypt to sell pumps. At a company he visited, the receptionist asked him for his name. He said it was Kirloskar.

'How strange', she said. 'Why is it strange?', he asked.

'Because the name of the pumps we buy is also Kirloskar!'

Here was a case of strong brand building, a name which was recognizable and which was respected, because the pumps were held in high regard. Never mind that the name of the founder was Laxmanrao Kirloskar, and his legacy is still continued in the fifth generation over 129 years. The power of genesis!

Source: *Balasubramanyam (2011)*

Liberalization: The New Era

The year 1991 was the turning point for the Indian economy with economic reforms and the advent of globalization. It was the period of economic transition, reforms and major policy changes. The government's objective was to make the economy fast growing and globally competitive. After Independence, the Licence Raj of almost three decades was dismantled and the 'scarcity economy' moved towards the free economy.

Indian industries and business houses protected by regulations and red-tapism suddenly faced the threat of extinction just like dinosaurs would have faced 65 million years ago. Many multinationals and transnational companies eying India's large middle-class segment of consumers were eager to set up shop with superior products, technology and deep pockets. The fear of survival with the onslaught of global competitors was across all, large-, medium- and small-sized companies.

By the end of the 1990s, the economic reforms were wide spread. Several giant organizations started the process of transformation. Some businesses realized that they did not have the capability to change or a drive to transform. Yet, there were many more, swift and agile to redefine their strategic intent, structures and resource allocation. They built competitiveness to survive and grab opportunities in a global business environment.

In 1998, *Business Today*, a prominent business magazine, surveyed India's top 50 business families, from the great empire builders such as Tata, Wadia, Kirloskar and Godrej to first-generation founding families such as Mallya, Ruia, Ambani and Dhoot. They were evaluated on four strategic parameters—business, family, structural capability and survival capability. The question was: Will Indian businesses survive the onslaught of the transnationals? Will India's 50 biggest business families manage to keep their conglomerates still at the top, 50 years down the line?

After 25 years of globalization, we find only 35% of these business houses have sustained, expanded and moved to the next level. Others have either exited, gone into oblivion or are sustaining without the glory of the yesteryears. Whether Mafatlal, Dhoot or Shriram families, the power and prominence these businesses enjoyed are now the stories of the past.

Marwaris have been India's most aggressive business community since industrialization. After economic reforms, although their dominance continued, the clout began to fail.

The relevance of business communities started diminishing. Community ties, which were important and gave tangible benefits in the past, were no longer relevant, as they did not give a competitive advantage either in providing seed capital or attracting managerial talent (Piramal 1999).

Entry of multinationals and foreign institutional investors encouraged Indian corporates to rethink on key issues and strategies. The family groups to be in the reckoning had to consider restructuring. Although some formed alliances to be globally competitive, others perished. With reforms, banks, foreign institutional investors, mutual funds and foreign brokers invaded the scene. But the late 1990s was a difficult period for businesses because of the competition from overseas. Many business houses, loss-making national banks and small-sector industries found it hard to survive in the globally competitive new millennium.

21st Century: The New Millennium

In the economic transition phase from 1990 to 2007, strategic planning was the mantra for growth for businesses which had a large span of operations and scope for growth. Most progressive business families restructured their businesses and organizations on the strategic business unit (SBU) model. The Internet and mobile telephony became a part of daily life. The social fabric of India changed with the rise of a 'new middle class' and an exploding consumer market that McKinsey Global Institute in 2007 described as India's 'bird of gold'.[4]

Conventional thinking and traditional practices of business in terms of finance, people and resource management required

---

[4]See http://www.bbc.com/news/world-asia-india-41264072, accessed 6 June 2018.

revamping. Trading and consumer-driven businesses struggled to keep pace with the Internet revolution and adapt to the world of digital. We entered the VUCA world with disruptions across technology, business models, leadership and strategies. The global community of investors, private equity funds and banks eyed the Indian markets. They entered as game changers, providing financial resources and partaking the ownership of the business.

In a changing scenario, the new economy—technology businesses—is a unique genre of commercial enterprises with never-before-seen valuations and fundings. Business families will have to take a quick call to adapt to the challenges of the new millennium, and aspirations of their millennial successors, while keeping the roots, the genesis of entrepreneurship, integral.

Musings

At the biennial award function of Marico Innovations in February 2018, a young 15-year-old boy from rural India, who had not yet finished high school, was given an award. He had developed a drone to identify landmines and also to neutralize them in situ. What a discovery! How many lives can be saved with this drone patented by this young man! Truly a product of the VUCA world which is moving with speed towards personal success and also major contributions to humankind.

THE START-UP WAY

At a lecture meeting on succession strategies for family businesses in Mumbai, about 60 family-business owners had gathered. Most of them were running small- and medium-sized enterprises. Most of them were first-generation founders. The topic of discussion continued on how to entice the gennext to join the family business.

Alok Gupta, a second-generation owner, aired his grievance,

> [A] lot of hard work and toil has gone into building my father's business. Now we are an ₹3 billion company, profitable with super potential to grow. But my son does not find it exciting to manage. He is a typical millennial and wants to become a social entrepreneur. I guess, business is in his genes, so he should succeed in his own venture.

Others nodded in agreement. The two different perspectives on Alok Gupta were intriguing. The father wanting the son to succeed, and the owner worried about the son's succession plan.

The succession scenario is changing. The practice of primogenial succession, the eldest son of the family to be the successor de jure, is changing. In the VUCA world, competencies and passions of younger members are important for being successors. The age of start-ups has set. It is the millennial's terrain, an interesting landscape.

India is going to be the world's youngest nation by 2020, with an average age of 34 years. Employment and employability will be a major challenge. Entrepreneurship is the buzzing career option. According to a report by NASSCOM and Zinnov, India is now the third-largest tech start-up hotspot in the world (Figure 1.3). Investment is rising, with the surge generating employment and providing solutions in areas from healthcare to agriculture (Myers 2016).

FIGURE 1.3 INDIA: FASTEST GROWING BASE OF START-UPS WORLDWIDE

The country has moved up to 3rd position and has the fastest growing base of start-ups worldwide...

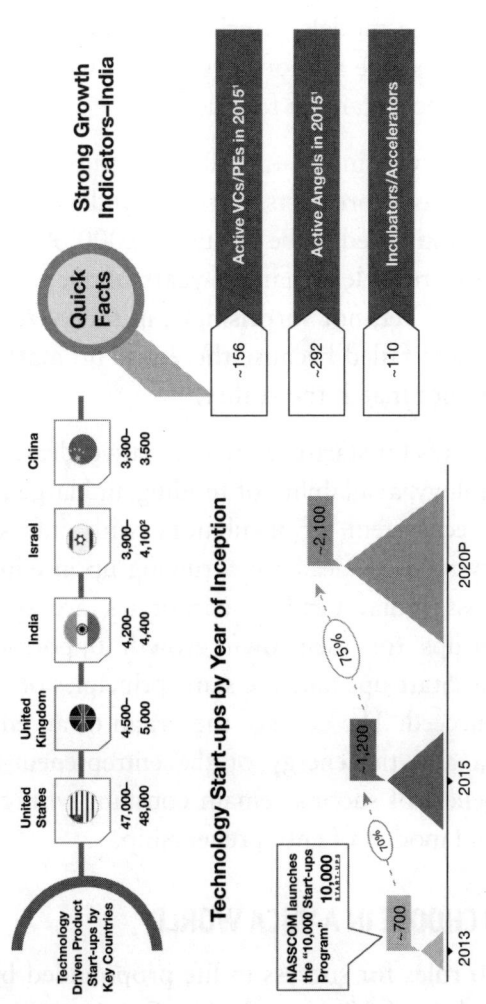

Technology Driven Product Start-ups by Key Countries

United States	United Kingdom	India	Israel	China
47,000–48,000	4,500–5,000	4,200–4,400	3,900–4,100[2]	3,300–3,500

Technology Start-ups by Year of Inception

~700 (2013) — 70% → ~1,200 (2015) — 75% → ~2,100 (2020P)

NASSCOM launches the "10,000 Start-ups Program" 10,000 STARTUPS

Quick Facts

Strong Growth Indicators–India

Active VCs/PEs in 2015[1]	~156
Active Angels in 2015[1]	~292
Incubators/Accelerators	~110

Source: Zinnov Research & Analysis, The Next Web, LeWeb Blog

Notes: [1] Active Angel (or VC/PEs) is defined as an investor who has made at least one investment in 2015
Presented numbers are for Jan-Sep 2015 period

[2] Number of tech start-ups in Israel have been estimated from the total number of start-ups in 2015 using % of tech start-ups in 2014

To be a founder, an innovator, a wantrepreneur is like receiving a badge of honour for millennials. The career choice of young scions is largely towards charting out their own path rather than working in the established business of their family. Their favourite role models, Mark Zuckerberg, Larry Page and Steve Jobs, became millionaires at less than 30 years of age. So why not be a start-up founder?

According to a survey[5] in 2014, 65,000 start-ups were floated in India for various products, services and industries. By 2020, they are estimated to be about 250,000. Almost 73% of the founders are of less than 36 years of age, and 6% of them are women. Yet, not surprisingly, in the maze of start-ups, 42% of them failed because there was no market need. The dream did not match the reality!

The growth drivers for start-ups are innovative ideas, access to suitable technology, availability of funding and large domestic markets. An ecosystem of incubators with infrastructure for technology-focused ideas are springing up in educational institutes across India. Leading corporates are sponsoring in-house start-ups for their own growth opportunities in new directions. Start-ups take the same principles of entrepreneurship to succeed. The genesis, the origin of an enterprise, is in the idea and the energy of the entrepreneur-founder. Values and beliefs of success remain constant with changing generations and models of entrepreneurship.

FREEDOM TO CHOOSE IN A VUCA WORLD

One of the 10 rules for success in life propounded by Cyrus Vance, the author of *Manager Today, Executive Tomorrow*

[5]See https://www.thequint.com/news/india/why-startups-not-small-industries-are-indias-salvation, accessed 6 June 2018.

(Vance 1974), is 'progress means different things to different people'. Do not use the achievements of others to measure your success. Each of us needs to set our own goals based on our capacity and capability. And then we have to measure ourselves against these goals. Each one is called to play a different role. If we play this well, to the best of our ability, we would not just be happy but also contented, doing what we like to do rather than what we have to do.

It was, therefore, somewhat distressing to read a headline in *The Times of India* of 11 December 2012—'IITians Struggle to Live Up to Families' Dreams'.[6] A student of civil engineering confessed that four years ago, when he qualified in the admissions entrance test JEE, his family members were thrilled and shared their joy that he would soon be earning in dollars. The pressure to live by their expectations was constantly weighing on him. It would seem that enough was never enough!

Another student who had just cleared the same entrance test wanted to do aeronautical engineering. But his ambitious and enthusiastic father did a quick survey of all the IIT departments and was put off by the average salaries offered to past students of aeronautical engineering, which according to him was poor compared to other departments. So he pushed his son into doing electrical engineering. Who knows? We might have lost an outstanding aeronautical engineer for an average electrical engineer!

There are many presumptions that mislead parents and students:

- That every IITian gets multiple offers, and is spoilt for choice
- That every IITian has a choice of working abroad

---

[6]See https://timesofindia.indiatimes.com/home/education/news/IITians-struggle-to-live-up-to-families-fat-pay-package-dreams/articleshow/17564282.cms, accessed 3 September 2018.

- That only technical skills and exam performance will bag them the best jobs
- That the highest salary got by one or two students is the average salary offered

None of these is true. It is only a few that may have the options. The others have to accept local jobs at lower salary packages and be happy that they are gainfully employed.

Unfortunately, the setting of unrealistic goalposts does not end with the first placement.

A vice president of one of the largest companies of a conglomerate in India applied for the position of president of a mid-sized company. He was asked in the interview why did he want to change the job. He was happy in his job, had climbed the ladder steadily over 20 years, was not unhappy with his company or the boss and was paid adequately by market standards. The answer was, 'most of my batch mates from the class of 85 have become presidents. I am still a vice president'. He was convinced to stay where he was and use his own measure of progress. He stayed, to later become the president of the same large conglomerate!

The concept of progress is quite wide. To some it can be helping others to progress, and to others it can be personal growth. Progress can be tangible in terms of physical comforts and better lifestyle. It can also be intangible in the form of 'contentment'. Any activity or enterprise done with passion and a sense of contribution to a larger environment can lead to 'contentment'—which money alone cannot buy. Problems of 'keeping up with Joneses' need not arise in the present VUCA world which has greater opportunities to achieve contentment.

FOUNDER'S FOOTPRINTS

A question that raises curiosity in every generation's entrepreneurs is, where did the big corporations of today come from? Nearly all of them evolved from the small business started by an individual or by a family of siblings or cousins. This is true for the Rockefellers and the Fords, for Walmart and Selfridges, and for Walt Disney and Goldwyn–Mayer.

Those who succeeded remunerated themselves and their families handsomely. Some part of the goodies were always shared with the stakeholders in the pipeline too. Not that it should cause disquiet or animosity, since they have taken large risks and might have possibly belonged to the 90% of entrepreneurs who fail, if not in the first year, then in the first three years. By succeeding, these entrepreneurs have contributed to the community, the society and to the country, and they deserve financial returns and rewards, within the legal framework of course.

It was therefore not surprising to see the results of a survey conducted by EMA Partners, commissioned by *The Times of India*. It showed that seven out of the top 10 women earners in India Inc. in 2013 belonged to the promoter group. The brigade was led by Kalavathi Kalanithi of Sun TV in South India, who earned nearly $10 million a year! All the others were at about $1.5 million a year or slightly lower.

The Economic Times also featured a list of the most eligible bachelors in the world—information sourced from the *Forbes* magazine of the USA. It means that these are not 'old billionaires'. Out of the five, only one—30-year-old Albert Fürst von Thurn und Taxis with a net worth of $1.6 billion— showed his source of wealth as 'inheritance'. The other four made money themselves, such as Drew Houston, the founder of Dropbox (30 years old; net worth $1.2 billion), Eduardo Saverin from Facebook (31 years old; net worth $4.1 billion), Robert Pera of Ubiquiti (35 years old; net worth $2.7 billion) and Yoshikazu Tanaka of Social Networking (37 years old; net worth $1.6 billion).

Fortune magazine compiled a list of the most admired companies in 2014,[7] a regular annual feature. A look at the top 10 shows that the founder still casts a shadow across the organization, even though the founder might have died some time ago. At least this is true of 9 out of the top 10 companies. And who are they? Starting from Apple as number one, others follow in sequence: Amazon, Google, Berkshire Hathaway, Starbucks, Coca-Cola, Walt Disney, FedEx, South West Airlines and General Electric.

Surveys and statistics on successful and wealthy entrepreneurs and successors indicate that the admiration of the company is high when the performance of the company is excellent, and when the connection with the founder and the family is still evident in the mindscape of the general populace. It is the footprint of the founder!

Spotlight on GENESIS

Harsh Mariwala, Chairman, Marico Limited, India.

Mr Mariwala is a third-generation scion of a business family, who joined the family business at the age of 20, after

---

[7]See 'Most Admired 2014', http://fortune.com/worlds-most-admired-companies/2014/, accessed 6 June 2018.

graduation, and then sought to strike a new path. With innovation, dedication and hard work, he built Marico into the sixth-largest Indian fast-moving consumer goods (FMCG) company with revenues of ₹60 billion. Marico, with brands like Saffola and Parachute, among others, that are household names has come a long way in less than 30 years.

Mr Mariwala talked about his journey. This will probably provide some guidelines, especially to the gen-next in family businesses and to entrepreneurs who are starting out 'de novo'.

The focus is on GENESIS—where he came from, how he started and changed direction and the rules he followed to make this achievement possible.

'My family was in the trading and distribution of oils and spices. I was the oldest male child of the third generation and the first to enter the business at the age of 20. Ours was a joint family. My father and my three uncles were then running the Bombay Oil Industries Ltd, which had made the transition from only trading to the manufacturing of oils, oleoresins, oleochemicals etc. The business was performing reasonably well.

However, I had a much larger dream. I believed there was an opportunity to build a branded consumer business. If MNCs could brand toothpaste and soaps, I knew that I could create a consumer franchise for high quality oils and other products too. I felt that not just manufacturing and distribution as we had been doing, but investments in marketing would pay dividends in the long run. I had the bug. I was eager to experiment.

I also realized that I would need to induct new talent into the company. At that time, our office in the congested Masjid Bunder area was not suitably located to attract professionals.

We would have to move elsewhere. In a few years' time, my younger cousins also joined the business. They too had their own dreams of building more valuable businesses. As the gen-next Mariwalas, my cousins and I began to build a consensus. The next step was to align the senior generation. Building consensus is important in joint families and family businesses.

It then took about three years to convince our seniors to allow our generation the independence to determine the future of the business we were given to manage with mentorship from our respective fathers. I took charge of the consumer products division of Bombay Oil and began to drive my strategy to make Parachute and Saffola consumer brands in earnest. I shifted the focus to consumer packs and began to reach out to new geographic markets. And the results were not only excellent but went beyond expectations. We reached a stage where 80% of Bombay Oil's turnover and close to 100% of the profit came from branded products. In order to build the mindset required of an FMCG company, and supported by the performance of the division, I was able to convince the family to house the consumer business in a separate company. In 1990, we set up a separate business, and Marico Industries was born'.

How did you manage to separate the business and yet maintain harmonious relations in the family?

'This is not easy. Because in a family business, it is all for one and one for all. Everyone is responsible, but few are accountable. Therefore, there was a great need to introduce systems. We had to rely on family confidants to help influence decisions, and we did. Now it is much easier because we have institutions of mentors and advisors who can smoothen the passage. But it was a different time.

In the early 1980s, we worked on a family constitution. It covered most areas—entry and exit norms, spending on cars, family dividend policy, and who will be spokesmen for the family and will get media exposure. Discussion, agreement and clear articulation play a critical role.

Importantly, we tried to create a culture of openness and trust, which is so necessary among family members. There are bound to be ego issues and conflict of view-points. But if there is a sense of fairness and equality, these issues get minimized. Processes were set for legal and taxation areas and to ensure transparent transactions. Then, there is no temptation for wrongdoing.

The organization

We five cousins headed the three different businesses of oils, chemicals and spices, but we were all equal owners. Accountability was distinct from ownership'.

It is said that Marico is among the best and professionally managed companies. How did you work out the transformation?

'At a very early age I realized that to build a great company, one needs to focus on building a great team that is talented and highly engaged. Value in an FMCG business is created through strong brands, and brand building is achieved only through people. The other key ingredient is innovation which can thrive if the right environment is created for it.

So for many years, I have worked at this. High levels of governance and an organizational culture of trust and meritocracy are essential to attract and retain professional management. I sought out people who were better than me in their area of expertise, and then empowered them. My role was to get the best out of the team. This also meant making sure that there is clarity of roles and, therefore, well-defined responsibilities and accountability. This enables proper performance management. Even today, I spend a lot of time with my teams, defining roles and bringing clarity.

I have seen too many disputes arising from cloudiness in this important area, and to a large extent, I think I have succeeded in clearing the air at regular intervals.

Because we have created a culture where professionalism and family business can comfortably coexist, Marico has been able to attract good talent. Professional managers, who are otherwise reluctant to join family companies (they suspect that they have to please their bosses all the time, and sometimes even their spouses who want to display ownership of the company), experience a meritocratic, vibrant and positive environment that provides professional challenge. This encourages them to give their best bringing their talent, analytical skills and process orientation to the table. This can then be married to the entrepreneur owner's sense of ownership, quicker decision-making and a grip on the business—call it *genetics?*

India is witnessing many young men and women taking to entrepreneurship. I will be happy if some of the thoughts I have shared help some of those who are at a stage where I was 30 years ago!'.

A DEBT OF GRATITUDE

On All Souls Day, Christians remember their ancestors and pray that their souls may rest in peace. Likewise, in every religion there is a remembrance—sometimes every day, sometimes once a year—to thank those who have left us, and before leaving, have made this world a better place for us to live.

Some communities have a practice of keeping aside food from the generous banquet served at a party for their dead ancestors. It may seem strange, because the dead cannot talk and obviously cannot eat! But it is the thought—a symbolic gesture of *thank you*—for whatever it may be worth in rational terms.

There is a long list of innovators whom we need to thank and who are seldom acknowledged. There are individuals who invented, gave the invention to the society and disappeared without building large corporations. Or there are entrepreneurs who built large corporations, and left a legacy from which their descendants benefited immensely. Or there could be those founders who went half the way to build the business, and then sold out or were taken over by someone bigger with resources and talent. Looking at such a list was a revelation, a great surprise!

- The pencil with eraser attached was developed by Hyman Lippmann. A great invention? NO. A useful invention? YES, as all of us are benefited.
- The safety razor was invented by King C. Gillette. From a single blade to twin blades, to three blades, to more?
- The drunkometer was invented by D. Rolla Harper, followed by the Breathalyzer by Robert Berkenstein. What would the police force do without this equipment anywhere in the world to manage drunken driving?
- The Yale lock (tumbler lock) was first created for banks in 1847 by Linus Yale Sr. It was adapted for use on other doors by Linus Yale Jr. Fortunately, they went on to the second generation of creativity!
- The pill that could easily be dissolved in the stomach (known as the friable pill) was invented by William Upjohn. Upjohn Laboratories had a long inning, and have now become part of the game of 'mergers and acquisitions'.

- Garrett Moran was given the first patent on a three-signal traffic light. And we never think of him or know about him as we cross signals 20 times a day.

- Frank Epperson was 11 years old when he invented the first popsicle in the world.

- Dr John Pemberton invented Coca-Cola in May 1886. The world praises the rise and rise of Coca-Cola. It was selected by *Fortune* magazine as the most admired brand in the world, after Job's Apple.

- Willis Habil and Carrier invented air conditioning in 1921. We still know, and at times buy, Carrier air conditioners nearly 100 years later!

- Eugene Polley invented the remote control in 1955. More than 50 years later, now we cannot imagine our lives without touching the remote control several times a day!

- John Curtis was the first to produce chewing gum on a commercial scale. While Singapore may have banned the use of chewing gum, the rest of the world goes chewing, at least on the pretext of 'fresh breath'.

- Jacob Davis invented blue jeans. And these are now a symbol of a world youth unified code for people from all parts of the world, even though mostly worn in the West, and mostly produced in China!

Of all these 'solos' who were the innovators and initiators, who opened new doors and showed new paths—our gratitude and respect from the 'large corporate' world. But for them, the corporates would not have been existing, whether in the East or the West. The large corporations today owe a debt to the founders and founding families of yesterday.

LOOK BACK TO LOOK FORWARD

Family businesses despite VUCA forces will not be outdated if their genesis, the foundation, is strong. But there is a danger that the spirit of entrepreneurship may get outdated if entrepreneurs and innovators stop learning from the past to anticipate the future.

We owe a debt of gratitude to innovators of the past, who built many large and small family businesses and have been the givers to the world in their innovative way. Entrepreneurs who are passionate about chasing a dream, to be successful, need to balance their passion with professionalism. As Dave Weinbaum, a well-known talk show host, has said, they have to 'learn the lessons from the past, to prepare for the opportunities of the future'.

Why Is Genesis the First G of the 5Gs?

We cannot erase the past. We cannot be a product of only the present and plan for the future. All of us are products of *nature* and *nurture*. Nature comes from Genesis. The past affects the present and the future. It determines our looks, our physique, our temperament, our likes and dislikes, our predilection to certain diseases, our value systems and our ethics, and much else. All this can be tempered and amended to some extent by individual effort. But it cannot be totally erased.

That is why, when I picked up the newspaper recently, when the World Cup matches had just begun in Russia, the headline screamed, 'Time for France to Show Pedigree'. Another newspaper the same day reported that there is going to be a gathering of thousands of people on World Environment Day at Stonehenge, a relic from prehistoric times that still stands tall in England. The Bible has its Book of *Genesis* and Hinduism has its Vedas that go back to thousands of years.

For better or for worse, we have to take cognizance of the past, review the present and plan for the future. In a VUCA world, the pace may change making everything faster. But the direction remains the same: always moving forward and making progress, to take humanity to the next level—generally for good and sometimes not so good.

The Roman god Janus, the god of beginnings and endings, and of doors and gates, who gave his name to the month of January, has two heads—one looking back and the other looking forward.

It is said that future-makers have three heads, one looking forward, one backward and one into themselves. They embrace what is called the destiny probe (insight), the future quest (foresight) and the wisdom search (hindsight).

By growing these capabilities, all of us can transform ourselves from a life as future-taker and path-taker to one of future-maker and path-maker. Many successful entrepreneurs do just this. They combine foresight to shape the future with insight and learn from hindsight.

Walter Vieira

2

GROWTH

The Never Ending Journey

" *Only those who will risk going too far, can possibly find out how far one can go.* "

T.S. Eliot

GROWTH: THE SECOND G OF THE 5Gs

In the early 1990s, the US Army War College described how the world would be like after the Soviet Union's collapse in a term—VUCA—which has turned out to be highly relevant for the military and for the business. The environment demands businesses to be prepared and anticipate changes, and be innovative and dynamic to mitigate risks of failure.

Growth is the key to the survival and sustenance of enterprises, especially when the average product life cycle has become 1 to 5 years in the digital era from 15 to 20 years in the pre-digital era. The volatility of nature and speed of change is profound—from IoT (Internet of Things) to fast-changing consumer preferences to big data analysis. We are finding economic scenarios uncertain and unpredictable—whether demonetization of Indian currency in 2016 or tax reforms in 2017 with the Goods and Services Tax (GST). The complexity of business operations and organizations has increased because of technology and automation. The reality of external environment is too hazy to anticipate what will happen next, and then comprehend the consequences of thoughts and actions.

Growth is not a choice, it is obligatory, being a crucial element of the 5G success framework for family businesses. It is a must to move ahead in the VUCA world. A company either grows or it stagnates or deteriorates and finally dies or changes hands. The process is the same for human beings as well as for groups of human beings constituting an enterprise like a family business.

The only difference is that unlike humans, companies can plan for, and manage to survive, for an extended period of time. As James C. Penny, the founder of JC Penney, has said,

'No company can afford not to move forward. It may be at the top of the heap today but at the bottom of the heap tomorrow, if it doesn't'.

THE LEADERS WHO FOLLOW TRADITIONS

The growth of a family business depends on how the family has learned from past experiences, how the organization has handled environmental jolts, how they have created the culture and encouraged innovation in succeeding generations, and how they have ensured that the money and power do not spoil the progeny, as it happens in many cases. There are many global examples of families like Ford and Cadbury, at the home front Mahindra, Bajaj and Ambani, where successors are trained to 'walk with kings without losing the common touch'.

Business is all about customers. The perception and understanding of who the customer is starts with the entrepreneur. Successful entrepreneurs know the wants, wishes, likes and preferences of their customers. They know the buying behaviour of their customers, and have an ability to listen to them and create a strong bond of trust with them.

There is a genre of businesses that choose a specific segment of product, stay with it and grow it, till they become specialists in their markets, nationally or globally. One such company is Serum Institute of India. Few know that they are the world's largest vaccine manufacturers, located in Pune, India, and owned by the Poonawalla family. The family came into the limelight because they bought the prized real estate property on the Mumbai seafront which was once a former palace of a maharaja of a princely state in India. The young CEO, Adar Poonawalla, also received the CNBC Asia Award for Corporate Social Responsibility in April 2018. The Poonawallas got known to the public more for these acquisitions than for the real business in which they are world leaders.

Another similar case is of the family that manufactures Angostura Bitters. The company Angostura Limited, founded by Dr Johann Siegert in 1830 in the Venezuelan town of Angostura, is the world leader in the 'bitters' business. Generations of the family have continued the business, and they package the product in the same outdated bottle and label which has become a trademark of this product. The winds of change with VUCA have not swept either Serum Institute or Angostura off their feet. They continue growing!

THE LEADERS WHO CHART NEW PATHS

There is another segment like Reliance Industries, who started with a textile mill and made the trademark of Vimal that is famous for their aggressive and effective advertising. They kept on with backward integration to manufacture polyester fibre, and further back to oil refineries and gas exploration. They kept moving on until the textile business now constitutes only a small portion of Reliance turnover. Reliance showed how to use imagination and ambition in business to create organic growth, with the expansion of business portfolios within the umbrella company. The Reliance revenues are estimated to be 2.25% of the GDP of India!

There are still other businesses that have ensured growth by keeping to the basic industry but changing strategies and technologies. Mahindra and Mahindra were once synonymous with Jeeps. First, they repaired them and then manufactured them. They moved on to SUVs and to tractors. Now the group is making efforts to be pioneers in the electric car business. Anand Mahindra has also managed to successfully foray into new areas as diversification, for example, in the IT industry with Tech Mahindra, and a partnership with Kotak group in the field of banking and finance.

Musings: To Succeed in Business, Know Your Customer

In 2012, the most admired 124-year-old manufacturer of film and cameras, Kodak, filed for Chapter 11 bankruptcy protection. In 2007, its stock price was $90 per share, and in January 2012, it plummeted to a miserable 76 cents. What happened to this coveted global brand that was once present in every home and office on earth?

As we look back on the history of Kodak, a picture of missed opportunities emerges. As customers were celebrating digital cameras and images, Kodak management stayed with traditional camera and film. Believing foolishly that its loyal customer base would never desert its famous product, a somewhat arrogant leadership of Kodak ignored Sony, Fuji and other innovative digital camera firms.

On the other hand, consider the crazy success of Skullcandy, a publicly traded company that sells amazing headphones to a specific target audience. A darling of investors and venture capitalists, it is showing consistently fast growth. What is the secret sauce for success?

The founder knows his customers. He truly understands the needs of individuals who want his funky products. His target audience ranges from 12 to 26 years of age. They are hip. They love music. He knows who they are, or want to be—cool, and accepted by their peers. He knows what they watch and where they shop. He knows what apps they have on their cellphones and iPads. Look around your neighbourhood at the youth on your street. They all have Skullcandy headsets or ear buds. Kids from every country on earth are wearing headsets with a skull on it.

Source: Hall (2012)

GROWTH: THE NEVER ENDING JOURNEY

Bajaj group ensured growth by getting out of the scooter market and getting into the faster growing motorcycle market, thus, taking the tide at the flood and moving forward—a case of disagreement between father and son, and the father allowing the son to use his judgement and take such an important strategic decision!

Others such as C.K. Ranganathan of CavinKare (Velvette shampoo) and Karsanbhai Patel of Nirma washing powder have taken advantage of the large consumer segment, 'the great Indian middle class' to manage steady growth. Incidentally, they have not duplicated their first product success in the same measure. The Shroffs of United Phosphorus, the largest manufacturers of phosphorus in India, went prospecting internationally and set up manufacturing plants in South America and other locations, ensuring high growth and profits by changing and expanding the geographical boundaries for their activities.

THE NON-MOVERS

All those who could not look back and learn from history, did not look sideways for opportunities and did not look forward to signs of new times are stagnating or have disappeared altogether from the business scene.

They remind us of the person for whom 'window is just a square hole in a room and application is something written on a paper', 'keyboard is a piano and mouse is just another animal', 'file is an important office stationery and hard drive is an uncomfortable road trip'. And for whom 'Apple and Blackberry are just fruits'. These are the leaders of family business who are no longer leaders because they have gone visionless and lost their way in a VUCA world. They cannot ensure the second G of the 5G success framework!

THE TORCHBEARERS

Family business is fascinating. We liken it to a single cell which then multiplies, enlarges and changes its form. Often it grows and, over a period, either transforms much beyond where it started or dies. The family business is where all economic activity starts, the compulsive initiative of an individual and the family to create a product or service to meet a need or a want, to fulfil a dream or an ambition, and in that process to build an enterprise.

In a way, an enterprise just happens. It evolves. The initial spark in the individual, over time, becomes a flame. The torch-bearer then tries to pass this torch to successors and then the following generations in the hope that the flame will never die. But it does. There are enterprises where the founder and founding generation's ethos are discarded soon after the flame is lit. And there are enterprises where the torch is carried forward for generations—15, 16 and sometimes more! The oldest family business on record in 2017 is a Japanese hotel, Hoshi Ryokan, owned and run by the same family since the year 718. The flame has continued since 46 generations.

HAND IN HAND TOGETHER: FAMILY-BUSINESS-OWNERSHIP

The family business is a complex system. Its life cycle is based on three dimensions: evolution of the family, dynamics of the business and structure of ownership. Each dimension has its own needs, goals, norms and membership rules (Gersick, Davis, Hampton and Lansberg 1997).

Families are governed by equality, inclusiveness and emotional bonding, be it the founding generation or succeeding generations. The level of trust, respect and sharing among members determine the harmony and cohesion of relationships. Family dynamics play a crucial role in the success and failure of family businesses.

The family's lineage and name, religion and community impact their choices of business. Whether the Palanpuri Jains from Gujrat having a monopoly on the global diamond trade, or the Bunt community from coastal Karnataka responsible for the growth of hotel industry—the community belongingness and social recognition are essential from a 'family' dimension.

Business has a logical and analytical approach. For growth, the vision of the leader, the organization's culture and the competencies play an important role. Transparency and merit in managing the business define its success and failure.

A family business is defined by family ownership more than the name of the family and number of relatives engaged in the business (Gersick, et al., 1997). There are many structures and distributions of ownership. For example, ownership along with management control is usually inherited by the succeeding generations, and at times, there are family and non-family investors who become a part of the ownership. Three types of ownership structures are common in family businesses: one is the single—a controlling owner—another is the partnership of siblings and the third is a group of cousins, also called Cousins Consortium (Ward 1991).

Family-business-ownership dynamics are complex and overlapping as each has a specific agenda: business is value driven—to customers and stakeholders; family is values driven—to preserve ethos, culture and genesis; and ownership is valuation driven—to gain the best market capitalization and return on investment. The equation of value–values–valuations has to be balanced to achieve growth—the second G of the 5G success framework.

Founder's values may not sustain over a time. Values may change and consequently, relationships and bonding among family members. Strategic and competitive advantages of the business change over a period and across markets. In a growing and evolving family business, the complexities are bound to increase. The vision and direction for growth, focus on results and long-term planning go a long way in balancing the three dynamics.

FAMILY IN BUSINESS OR BUSINESS FAMILY?

Alas! An intriguing thought for family businesses! It triggers a discussion and debate all the time. For some families, it is the business that serves the needs of the family, and some families serve the business as executors and trustees of a legacy. Some families set clear boundaries between family and business matters and tend to be more business first. Some families give importance to needs of the family over what is best for the business. For them 'family first' is the ethos to the fore (Reid 1999).

Researchers Leenders and Waarts (2003) studied competitiveness and performance management of different types of family businesses. They selected criteria such as trust, social control, motivated employees, management control, conflict resolution, continuity and atmosphere to evaluate and compare companies' performance. Based on these criteria, they made a distinction between a company's family orientation and business orientation (Figure 2.1).

FIGURE 2.1 THE FAMILY BUSINESS SPACE

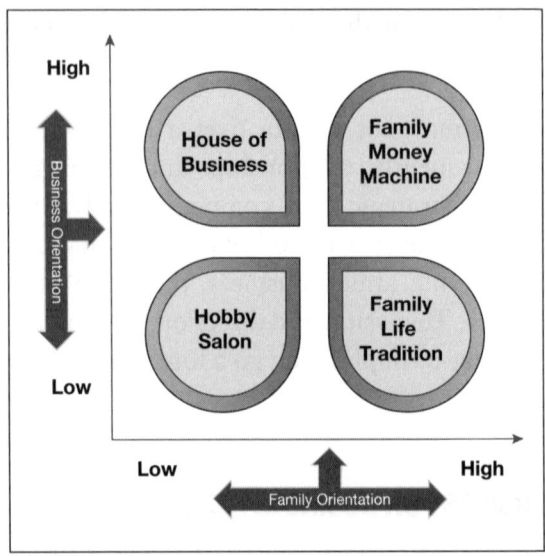

Source: Adapted from Leenders and Waarts (2003)

Family Money Machine

The companies with strong family as well as business orientation are the ones that show a strong performance drive and also harmonious family relationships. Researchers have named them as *Family Money Machine.* For these firms, business value creation and family togetherness both are important. Business continuity is ensured through strategic decisions on products, markets, capital and organization. The ownership control remains with the family, and management is by professionals. In the Indian context, Godrej and Murugappa families would belong to this category.

House of Business

Another type of companies has high business orientation compared to family orientation. These are called *House of*

Business. Management and ownership in these companies are separated, and the family's approach towards business is professional and clearly defined. The examples could be Dabur and Asian Paints where family members are not a part of the management. Professionals manage the business with complete freedom. Family members may be on the board of directors to provide only strategic inputs.

Family Life Tradition

The family could be of multiple generations or of single, a joint family of siblings and cousins, or a nuclear family. When the members, the owner-managers, are intensely involved in managing the business, it falls into the category of *Family Life Tradition*. The family's needs and aspirations get priority over business objectives. At times, business decisions are compromised to keep family members satisfied. Businesses falling in this category would find it difficult to adapt to VUCA challenges and need to introspect their position for long-term survival. In our experience, majority of small- and medium-sized enterprises (SMEs) in India belong to this category.

Hobby Salon

Families running businesses to earn a living, to meet their lifestyle expenses or to keep themselves occupied fall in the category of *Hobby Salon*. These are usually small, marginal businesses, driven by one or two individuals. They cannot sustain a growing family, and successors may not find it attractive to work in the business unless there is a possibility of growth or diversification. We come across businesses which were reputed and prosperous once upon a time, but with family feuds, divisions or lack of succession planning, the businesses became marginal and almost extinct.

SHIFTING GEARS

According to Arie de Geus (1997), most commercial corporations are underachievers. At the founding stage, they are in the early phase of evolution. They develop and exploit only a small fraction of their potential. Their mortality rates are high and premature. It is not surprising to find almost 50% start-ups failing in the first five years. For family businesses as well, the growth journey is not consistent; whether it be the founding or succeeding generations, keeping the business thriving for a long time is difficult. The history of business corroborates the fact. For example, one-third of the 1970 *Fortune* 500 companies were acquired or broken into pieces, or had merged with other companies by 1983.

There is another side. Businesses have lasted and thrived for centuries, across generations. Globally there is evidence of greater corporate longevity. Japan's Sumitomo has its origins in a copper-casting shop founded by Riemon Soga in 1590. And the Swedish company Stora, a major paper, pulp and chemical manufacturer, began as a copper mine in central Sweden more than 700 years ago. Such examples suggest that it is possible to have a natural lifespan of a corporation as two or three centuries—or more (de Geus 1997).

When the economy was liberalized in 1991, India's family businesses ensconced in a protective Licence Raj were suddenly exposed to the threats of global competition. The attrition rate of non-progressive family businesses increased. At the same time, growth opportunities were unleashed. Banking, telecom, IT and infrastructure opened up for the private sector.

The economic reforms gave an impetus to the churn—the old order gave way to the new. Bharti, Adani, GMR, JSW and

Jaypee group are the products of post reforms. With the global software boom in 2000, Infosys and Wipro entered the top-20 league.

The table 'India's Top 20 Business Groups by Assets' (rediff.com 2016) depicts the top 20 groups ranked according to their assets from 1951 to 2016, a period of 65 years. Only three

INDIA'S TOP 20 BUSINESS GROUPS BY ASSETS

	1951		1990		2016
Rank	Business Group	Rank	Business Group	Rank	Business Group
1	Tata	1	Tata (Exd ACC)	1	Tata
2	Birla	2	Birla	2	Mukesh Ambani
3	Martin Bum	3	Ambani	3	Birla AV
4	Sahu Jain	4	J.K. Singhania	4	Anil Ambani
5	Bird Hilgers	5	Thapar	5	Vedanta
6	Andrew Yule	6	Mafatlal	6	Bharti
7	Shriram	7	Bajaj	7	L&T
8	Mafatlal	8	Modi	8	Adani
9	Kasturbhai Lalbhai	9	M.A. Chidambaram	9	HDFC
10	J.K. Singhania	10	TVS	10	Mahindra
11	Walchand	11	Shriram	11	ICICI
12	Thapar	12	UB	12	OP Jindal
13	Bangur	13	Bangur	13	JSW Group
14	Khatau	14	Kirloskar	14	Jaypee Group
15	Indra Singh	15	Walchand	15	Infosys
16	Seshayee	16	Mahindra	16	Wipro
17	Ramakrishna	17	Goenka	17	DLF
18	Kirloskar	18	Nanda (Escorts)	18	Axis Bank
19	Mahindra	19	Lalbhai	19	GMR
20	Shapoorji	20	Ruia (Essar)	20	Rahul Bajaj

Source: http://www.rediff.com/money/report/special-in-india-15-of-the-top-20-business-groups-are-family-owned/20160818.htm

business groups that were among top 20 in 1951—Tata, Birla and Mahindra—are still in the table. Sixteen of the top 20 business groups in 2016 are products of the post-Independence economic growth. They now account for two-thirds of the combined assets and nearly 70% of the combined revenues of the top 20.

'Family businesses that make it through many decades and even centuries, are the ones who are strong in their genesis, the values and have developed a personality', says Arie de Geus. 'They know who they are, understand how they fit into the world, value new ideas and new people and husband their money in a way that allows them to govern' (de Geus 1997).

The genesis of the longevity of family businesses lies in its success of managing family dynamics positively and smoothly. The unity and cohesiveness of the family, the strength of the alliance and a shared vision lead to continuous growth (*Tharawat Magazine* 2013). There were large groups such as Walchand, Mafatlal and Khatau who found it difficult to cope up with structural changes. They could not retain the top 20 position. Incoherence and disputes among family members might be the raison d'etre for the fall!

GROWING IN VUCA ENVIRONMENT

Growth is a necessity. Like with humans, we need to extend the period of anabolism and reduce the period of catabolism. Once the cycle of growth reaches its peak, it may be time to start another cycle and thus keep moving on.

Family businesses have adopted various routes for growth. Some successors have continued to follow the business started by the founders—their fathers or grandfathers—and have grown substantially. Others have diversified into new segments, products and global markets. Some have as entrepreneurs created own footprints in developing first-generation conglomerates. Irrespective of their size and industry, the contribution of family businesses in India's growth is commendable.

Growth cannot happen without challenges. According to the PwC India Family Business Survey 2016 (PwC 2016) market conditions, government policies and regulations, innovation, digital disruption, technological changes, attracting and retaining talent, competition and professionalization were the challenges faced by almost all the businesses. In the survey, 56% of Indian family businesses felt that the 'need to innovate' will be a key challenge in the next five years—35% had planned to transfer management to the next-gen; 48% had planned to retain ownership but bring in professional management. And surprisingly, only 15% of family businesses had a robust, documented and communicated succession plan.

PREPARING FOR VUCA

The VUCA environment has impacted family dynamics in family businesses. Feuds and splits in prominent business families such as the Ambani brothers, Bajaj cousins, Mafatlal in-laws and Hiranandani father and daughter clearly indicate lack of unified vision, divergent beliefs and values, and transparency among family members.

Creating a culture of governance to deal with conflict, preparing the next-gen and planning for succession are the key aspects where business families have to develop aptitudes and capabilities. Family businesses of the 21st century will require new skill sets. They will require talents to navigate through the maze. The leaders of the family or professionals will have to become VUCA ready (Naidu 2014).

Research says that the companies whose leaders are trained for VUCA environment are 3.5 times more likely to succeed than those with low VUCA capability. Some of the core skillsets for VUCA enablement are:

- Far-sightedness and the ability to picture the future scenario of economic, political and environmental forces
- Cognitive and soft skills to deal with diverse employees, millennials and techies
- Motivation and encouragement for creativity and innovation
- Remaining flexible and taking advantage of technology
- Hunger to learn, humility to listen to stakeholders and ability to inspire themselves

Since Independence, businesses in India have gone through several disruptive phases in the economy. With the biggest tax reform of GST, India's $2 trillion economy is going through massive market reforms. The future is for those business groups which will focus on their core competencies and go for global markets. Those who will embrace the change and shift gears will continue to grow, while others will fall off the racing track.

THE NEED FOR PASSIONALS, NOT JUST PROFESSIONALS

Businesses—family and otherwise—have grown and prospered when the leaders have been passionals—not just professionals! Whatever business experts may say, we find the most important distinguishing factor between the founder-leader and professionals is the factor of passion.

We often talk facilely about the discovery of electricity and how Edison changed the way we live. We don't talk about the fact that he conducted over 10,000 experiments before he discovered electricity. Surely, there must have been times when he felt like giving up, when he felt he was a loser. But he persisted because he had passion.

Musings

On returning home one evening, I found my grandchildren, aged eight and seven, lying on their backs, under the dining table. What were they doing? I asked them. They said that they had been taught at school that day about Michelangelo and how he had painted the Sistine Chapel at the Vatican St. Peter's Church. Lying on his back for months on end, painting the great scenes on the ceiling, balancing on ropes. Now my grandchildren were trying to do likewise and had stuck papers to the underside of the dining table, and found it extremely difficult.

'Grandpa, how did Michelangelo do it?', they asked. I thought about an answer for a long time. The simplest answer was—Michelangelo had talent and passion. That is how he could make it happen. And we see the result even so many centuries later!

Walter Vieira

At the age of 65, Colonel Sanders started Kentucky Fried Chicken which he had developed using herbs and spices that made fried chicken different and tastier than anything that existed before. He then took samples and went around the country offering a franchise for his product. As the story goes, he heard 1,009 'no's' before he heard his first 'yes'.

Why did he do this? Was this necessary at the age of 65 when he had retired, and he could have just put his feet up and rested? But for Colonel Sanders, it was *passion*. He, therefore, went on to build Kentucky Fried Chicken into one of the icons of America and worldwide, in the league of McDonalds and Coke.

It is said that Michael Dell went back to Dell Computers, the company he had founded, when he learned that it was floundering just two years after he had quit total control. He could not let it sink. He had built it, starting with an innovative idea and with passion. He wanted to bring it back to its past glory—and it was not for the sake of just personal gain!

Howard Schultz of Starbucks went back after seven years to take over as CEO (a post he had relinquished in 2000), although he need not have. When Starbucks began to falter, he decided to take charge again as CEO and bring it back to its past glory. And he did. In that process, he took care of his customers as his priority, his employees as his second priority (where he gave medical cover even to temporary employees) and finally the shareholders.

One more example is of Jim Sinegal, the co-founder of Costco, who took care of his employees and paid them more than market wages, encouraged long-term association, and built a business model where customers get the best deal and an easy 'return if not satisfied' policy. Sure, Wall Street has been critical of him for following an 'over-charitable' employee policies when he could have shown better net profits than 2% of the turnover. But for Jim, Costco was a *passion*. It was not just about Wall Street and the market price of the stock!

Non-family professionals are although obliged to play a different game. They march to the beat of a different drummer. The drummer is Wall Street, or the stock exchange or the outside investor in different parts of the world. If the stock price keeps rising, quarter after quarter, they are successful. If the price does not keep rising, they are looked upon with a frown by both Wall Street and their board. The number of CEOs who keep losing their jobs over short tenures is increasing rapidly. Yahoo has had six CEOs from 1995 to 2012 until the stabilizing factor of Marissa Mayer came on the scene, and Yahoo shares have begun showing an upward trend.

Sure, there are long-term CEOs like Jack Welch of GE and Alfred Sloan of GM, who are identified with the company and its philosophy. But one may still doubt whether they can cultivate the same passion as the founder would do. That very subtle distinction will always lurk, in spite of protestations!

FAMILY BUSINESS NEEDS ACHIEVERS

The entrepreneurs, the founders of family businesses, are loners, who seek to fulfil a dream. They have passion and in the manifestation of that passion, they make our world change. It may be in small yet profound ways—like a Hyman Lipman developing a pencil with a tipped eraser, or a Henry Ford developing a conveyor system to manufacture automobiles more economically, and grandly pronouncing that the customer can have any colour of car, provided it is black.

Dr Adele Scheele, in her research on mapping lives of successful people, divided the world of professionals into two groups: Sustainers and Achievers (Scheele 2004). It is said that Sustainers represent 80% of our workforce. They are the ones just doing their jobs well, and waiting passively for recognition, praise, raises and promotions. The other 20% are Achievers, who do not only do well but also actively seek both recognition and opportunity. They network with people, build contacts and alliances, and take risks to advance their careers.

Family businesses have been started by Achievers since time immemorial. Over 60% of the trade in most countries is accounted for by small and medium sized family businesses and start-ups. That is why governments emphasise promoting them with incubation and financial support. They realize that these family businesses form the foundation of a strong national economy and give an impetus to new ventures.

The furious forces of VUCA environment have impacted the performance and longevity of family businesses. The spirit of enterprise in India is never dying. *Business Today* conducted a survey of India's top family businesses in 2011, after 20 years of globalization, and listed top-ranked, century-old companies. Started by entrepreneurs, all these companies in the course of time had become giant enterprises and business houses. These companies are still surviving and adapting to the VUCA environment. From 36 companies who are in existence for over 100 years, 15 companies have responded well to the change. The table, '100+ and Not Out: The Growth Legacy of India's Family Businesses' (*Business Today* 2011) lists these 15 companies.

100+ AND NOT OUT: THE GROWTH LEGACY OF INDIA'S FAMILY BUSINESSES

1.	Bennett, Coleman & Co: Just in times (1838)
2.	Britannia: Not by bread alone (1892)
3.	Century Textiles & Industries: Century's century (1897)
4.	CESC: Power to the people (1897)
5.	Dabur: Growth energizer (1884)
6.	Godrej & Boyce: Safe and sound (1897)
7.	Indian Hotels: Halls of fame (1902)
8.	ITC: Imperial touch (1910)

9. Kirloskar Brothers: Pump and show (1888)
10. Shalimar Paints: Paintmaker iconic (1902)
11. Tata Steel: Nerves of steel (1907)
12. TVS: Cruise control (1911)
13. Jessop & Company: Grandpa of them all (1788)
14. Bombay Dyeing: Reinventing itself (1879)
15. DCM: Hopes to thrive again (1909)

BEWARE OF THE ONE PERSON COMPANY: EVEN GROWING SUCCESSFULLY!

When we talk about family business, we think about a family, and even about two or three generations. But there are times when we encounter a one-man institution. A person who has the intellect and the capability to build a business just by himself, and make it significant, even international. There is no succession. And there can be no clone. No one else can do what this one person can do, and does.

Such a one is Warren Buffett. He has built an empire—Berkshire Hathaway—all by himself. It has been done brick by brick. Sometimes going against the grain and against the sense of many of his shareholders. But he has proved himself right in the long run. Especially during and after the dot-com bubble!

How will Berkshire Hathway do after Warren Buffett? The trait Buffett is looking for in Berkshire's next CEO: *The new boss shouldn't be in it for the money.* It is said that Warren Buffett has trained and anointed Ajit Jain as his successor, who will later carry the company flag. A large number of shareholders, who are also Buffett fans and admirers, will be waiting to see how this works!

With a professional output which involves only the intellect and keen judgement of an individual, it is difficult for others to either greatly contribute or to participate. In fact, participation can be dangerous and risky.

Some years ago, an eminent quality management consultant floated an associate company to deal with projects. Three of his friends invested a sizable capital in a new private limited company. Three years later, the capital had eroded by 50%. The CEO, the chief promoter, had been drawing his slice of emoluments and expenses, not concentrating on results. The sales were poor and the losses kept mounting every year. At one point of time, the remaining investors felt it was enough. They pulled out with half of the capital invested, making a loss of hard-earned money. There was no recourse. It was a dependence on the expertise of *one* person, and this can be very risky. The investors had made a mistake in not taking such dependency into account when they decided to invest—the old story of all 'eggs in one basket!'

It is not for nothing that even large consulting firms, or law firms or medical polyclinics, are not open to general investors. Only those who can contribute expertise have a share in the firm. The shareholding ceases when the contributor leaves. It is not an association for a lifetime, and there is no opportunity for family succession. It is the here and now! A constantly flowing stream of 'present contributors'.

It is a different kind of family business which is not for all the family, but only for that part of the family that can contribute, and only when they do contribute! All the others who are looking for investment opportunities and growth of their wealth had better stay away.

A BOOSTER DOSE OF ENTREPRENEURSHIP TO CHANGE DIRECTION

Growth is vital yet tricky. In a world rapidly changing with technology, with cloud computing and the IoT, there are family businesses that come to the crossroads and sometimes even face a blank wall. It happens that the business of the past is no longer attractive as a business of today, and will perhaps not exist as a business of the future. It is where the challenge arises for the successive generations of the entrepreneur family.

Western India Vegetable Products Limited (Wipro) was a mid-sized, prosperous company that manufactured hydrogenated oil. It was probably the largest in the category since it was the supplier to Unilever India, who branded and sold its product as their flagship product—Dalda. It was the branded cooking oil most widely used in India—and better known than the name of the parent company.

However, this cooking medium was coming under the radar of 'unhealthy foods' as a cause of high cholesterol levels.

Young Azim Premji came back from the USA, midway through his studies after the sudden death of his father, to take charge of the family business. Did he see the writing on the wall and the sentiment against hydrogenated oil and such products in the future? During the 1970s, he decided to change the focus from oil to assembling computers. Since this was an embryonic industry, he poached knowledgeable personnel from DCM, a pioneer who had put together a fine team. Wipro expanded from hardware to software and is now ranked among the top three software companies in the country. The turnover is perhaps a thousand times what it was in cooking oils. Azim Premji is listed among the 10 richest men in India. Although the name of the company remains the same—Wipro—and they do not sell any oil; what they now do is a far cry from what they did in earlier generations. And now they need not explain what the name Wipro stands for!

Another company was Bombay Oil Industries in the business of trading of commodities including coconut oil. It was owned by three generations of the Mariwala family in Mumbai, India. In the 1970s, the third-generation scion, Harsh Mariwala, was bitten by the marketing bug and concepts of branding, segmentation and positioning. He wanted to upgrade the business. He was sure that the company's profits would be much higher by branding the products rather than selling in an undifferentiated market of commodity trading. Senior-generation members did not agree initially, and then saw the merit of his business model. Forty years ago, he worked out a fair settlement and parted ways to chart his course. Today, Marico Industries Ltd is among the leading FMCG companies in India with branded products such as Parachute coconut oil and Saffola, low cholesterol sunflower cooking oil. With other offshoot ventures such as Kaya Skin Clinics, Marico is spreading its wings internationally, and is leaving its footprint in Africa and Southeast Asia.

Sometimes, younger generations look for different directions outside the industry they had inherited, like Wipro, or within the industry, like Marico. Either way, if they have made a big success, we can label it as *booster dose entrepreneurship!*

Wise Leader: A Key for Growth

A commonly held belief is that to become a better leader, one has to improve their performance at work. Robert Rosen, a leadership expert, believes that to be a leader today, one has to be healthy, wealthy and wise. He is the founder of Healthy Companies International and the author of *'Grounded: How Leaders Stay Rooted in an Uncertain World'*.

Rosen presents another point of view: '[W]ho you are as a human being, is what drives you at the workplace, and that will determine how well you perform'. Rosen has spent two decades studying how to build better companies that balance results with the human side of the business. Having studied leaders, he noticed two things. One is that the world was changing faster than the ability of leaders to reinvent themselves, and another is the model of leadership. It is based on the paradigm that what you do as a leader, drives you as a person.

According to Rosen, the combined forces of competition, complexity, constant change and information overload, all work together to box in the leader. The leader's response to the crisis will determine how he and the company he runs will perform. Here is where healthy leaders are needed who are disciplined, self-aware and committed to personal growth for themselves and all those around them. They are attuned to four agendas: the *financial* agenda ensures that they have the capital and the results required for success and growth; the *operations* agenda that is focused on efficiency and processes; the *market agenda* which keeps them tuned to customers and competition; and, most important, the *human* agenda.

The late Dini Gaitonde was the president of Century Enka, a highly successful BK Birla group company in the production of synthetic fibre. There used to be snide remarks about Dini spending more time out of the office than in the office. He was out to see employees in the hospital, to help with the admission of their children to better schools where 'influence was important' and to talk to specialist doctors about improved medical treatment for special problems of employees. But Dini was a CEO who was not only admired but was also loved.

One day, as the story goes, he was surprised that the chairman's son, Aditya Birla, who ran his clutch of highly successful companies, phoned him. Aditya told him that he had met a very fine and personable young banker at one of his meetings and thought he would be a good match for Dini's daughter. Dini was touched that Aditya had the time and inclination in an altogether busy life to even think about Dini's daughter. Aditya offered to host a small party at his own home so the two families could meet. It was a most enjoyable evening. The young couple liked each other, and after a brief courtship, they were married.

It is the story of an owner of a multi-billion dollar family business, who had a human agenda. And a story of a high ranking professional manager, who also had a human agenda. And the bonds that are created through genuine concern and caring to connect the two successful leaders even in these turbulent times.

Source: *Grounded: How Leaders Stay Rooted in an Uncertain World*, Bob Rosen *(San Francisco, CA: Jossey-Bass, 2014)*

PROFESSIONALIZING: A NECESSITY IN A VUCA WORLD

It is often said that one of the key challenges of family businesses is to professionalize their work culture to ascertain long-term success and competitiveness. Integrating traditions and values of business families into a system promoting meritocracy however, does not happen in a day and certainly does not happen easily.

Abdullah Al Majdouie, President of the Almajdouie Group, Saudi Arabia (*Tharawat Magazine* 2010), gave an honest and most practical account of the changes his family business went through and the conditions for a successful change.

In an interview, he mentioned,

> [T]he history of our business dates back to the mid-1960s. More specifically, it began in 1965 when our founding father, Sheikh Ali bin Ali bin Ibrahim Al Majdouie was a truck owner. Inspired by the values drawn from the tolerant teachings of Islam emphasising dedication, perseverance and work accuracy, our founder was aware of the significance of these values for winning the trust of clients and continuity of work, be they large or small companies. More importantly, he managed to instil this spirit and values in his entire team of supporters and workers at the time. Until today, trust, dedication and perfection have been the underlying pillars for the Group's work and the guiding principles for its prosperity and growth. Today, the group is a large conglomerate with several businesses in logistics, automobiles, industries, and properties and investment with subsidiaries and branches. The Almajdouie group currently employs approximately 5,000 employees.

Abdullah Al Majdouie said,

> Through broadening business activities and growth in human capital, the group expanded its operation over Saudi Arabia and the GCC countries. This expansion made the family-run modus operandi hardly sufficient to guarantee work progress. The third generation is about to become active in the business, and there is a call for shifting over from the individual based work system to a rigorous governance efficient system conducive to pushing the wheel of growth forward and maintaining the company's customary level of performance for its clients.[1]

---

[1]See http://www.womeninfamilybusiness.org/professionalizing-family-bus-majdouie/#gs.Tgz49mg, accessed 12 September 2018.

THE PROFESSIONAL CULTURE

Managing business professionally with the help of non-family professionals instead of catering to the whims of the family is one of the key changes that has happened due to economic reforms. For growth, companies have to respond to multiple challenges such as competing in global markets, being agile and adaptive to new management techniques, and developing impeccable systems and processes. In family-run businesses, the family's power of ownership allows it to pursue its objectives and aspirations, regardless of the management and organization framework. The organizational culture is determined by the founder's and family's values. In professional culture, ownership and management are treated as two separate systems. Business decisions are not influenced by the family's personal agenda.

Professional managers often bring with them a set of assumptions that are different from those of the owners. Professionals' stance towards employees is rather impersonal and objective. Their belief and comfort are in working with processes and systems. Transparency and above-board transactions are the features of professionalism. Professionalizing a business, simply put, is managing the business with the help of executives who have received formal education, have subject matter expertise and have rational perspectives. Competence and performance take precedence over loyalty and relationships.

The trends are changing. Gen-next scions of business families are educated abroad and are trained to manage complexities of their business professionally. Whether Kumar Mangalam Birla or Mukesh Ambani, Anand Mahindra or Rajiv Bajaj, the successors are now professional family members giving a new dimension to family-business-ownership dynamics.

Musings: Growth Tonic

Tension suddenly crept in during a quarterly review meeting at Dabur in January 2009. A young manager walked up to the chairman, Anand Burman, with a tray of new mint-flavoured Hajmola candies that would soon be launched. Burman popped one into his mouth, but spat it out within seconds. 'It is awful. No one can eat this stuff', he said.

Complete silence followed. Plans for the launch were ready. What would happen now? Only CEO Sunil Duggal remained unfazed. 'What do the research results show', Anand asked the manager who had brought the candies. The feedback had been positive, he was told. 'We are launching it next month', Duggal announced. True to his word, Hajmola Mint was launched within a month. It went on to record ₹80 million in revenue within the first year.

Not a well-known story, but it is heard every time employees are asked why they stay with Dabur. 'The cornerstone of our growth is the empowerment of employees', says Duggal. 'We are allowed to take risks, innovate and sometimes even fail'. The genesis of Dabur is in the professional culture and trust in employees.

Source: *Pande (2011)*

AGILITY AND ABSORPTION: TOUGH DECISIONS

Characteristics of Leaders

The start-up phase and the first decade of an enterprise is normally a high growth phase, before a period of temporary stability sets in. This period needs leaders who can take tough decisions.

In the *Harvard Business Review* of February 2009, Donald Sull (2009) wrote about the two essential characteristics of great entrepreneurs—*Agility and Absorption*. Agility was characterized as 'floating like a butterfly and stinging like a bee' whereas Absorption was described as 'taking a licking and still keep kicking'. Sull then applied these characteristics to two yesteryear boxing legends. George Foreman was the reigning heavyweight champion. He was a giant of a man. He had *Absorption*. Challenging him was Mohammad Ali, a man with great *Agility*. It was the fight of the decade, held in Zaire in Africa, with the whole world focused on what was labelled as Rumble in the Jungle. The prize for the winner was $10 million, a huge sum in those days.

Business founders and leaders unfortunately cannot be like boxers, focused on agility or absorption. They need to have both these qualities. They need to float like butterflies and sting like bees, and take a licking and yet keep ticking. These qualities distinguished the founders of path-breaking companies known worldwide—FedEx, Walt Disney, IBM, Siemens, Merck, Johnson and Johnson, and many others. Besides these two qualities that served as the foundation, they surely had other qualities which were essential for their business growth—technical ability for Ford, creative ability for Walt Disney, software savvy for Gates and the list goes on.

Can this combination of +2 always be transferred genetically? Can the founder ensure that the next generation has the +2, a necessity to carry on the work that has been done by the founder of the enterprise? It is for the founder to be ruthlessly clinical in assessing whether any of his children meet the criteria. It is not easy. It requires great courage to say *yes*. It requires even greater courage to say *no*.

The Growth Mindset

It is this 'greater courage' that made Lord Leverhulme admired by many, as a business icon. The founder of Unilever started with Sunlight soap to build today's giant FMCG company Unilever. He had a huge placard facing his desk, which said, 'management consists of doing simple things; doing them regularly, and never forgetting to do them'. He always abided by this principle that helped him immensely.

Lord Leverhulme also decided that after his retirement, the company would be managed by 'professionals' and not by his two sons. He assured his sons that they will inherit the shares, and the company will do much better and so will they if it was managed by the professional managers he had identified. Family members have kept themselves away from the business and still enjoy the benefits of excellent growth by being the shareholders. It would not be surprising if the current generation of Lord Leverhulme's family, undoubtedly so wealthy, may not even know the turnover or span of operations of Unilever worldwide!

In the family business, these are tough decisions to be made, requiring one to be cold and clinical with one's kith and kin. While this may be unpleasant, it is a necessity. To the two essentials for entrepreneurs, a third must be added—fair judgement. It is for the good of the organization and the whole team, rather than only for the good of the individual and his immediate family.

If all three essentials are present, it is the best combination that a family business can have. And these family businesses are truly blessed! They will continue to grow just like Unilever has.

Musings

There is a story told about Andrew Carnegie, the steel baron of the USA, who built an empire from scratch and whose life story is like a fairytale! It is said that he wanted to select a personal assistant and requested his manager to go through the process of identifying a possible candidate who fit the job description. Only the final two were to be sent to Carnegie.

At the final selection, they were identified and sent. Carnegie gave each one an identical box tied with a ribbon. He asked them to go to different rooms and bring him the message in the final box, and as soon as possible. They went away. One had used scissors to cut the ribbon of one box inside another (such as 10 boxes) and quickly got to the smallest box and the inconsequential message. He went back to Carnegie. The other candidate was systematic. He untied ribbons, kept the boxes one over the other, and took many minutes more to get back to Carnegie.

Carnegie explained to his manager who was shocked at the selection of the first candidate. 'We have now come to a period where we must save time—not strings', he said simply and firmly.

A Tale of Two Brothers: ACG Continues to Grow

Ajit Singh, Chairman, ACG Worldwide (the Associated Capsules group of companies)

Success stories are always interesting, and some are inspiring. Ajit Singh and his brother Jasjit Singh are known as the Capsules Czars. Ajit Singh shared his views on the success of his family business and the owners' growth mindset.

The story of Jasjit and Ajit Singh reminds one of the quotes from James Allen:

> 'Dream lofty dreams, and as you dream, so shall you become. Your vision is the promise of what you shall one day be. Your ideal is the prophecy of what you shall at last unveil'.

'For over 50 years, my brother Jasjit and I have managed to work in harmony and transform our small organization into a leading international player.

One of the reasons for our success is our unusual upbringing. During most of our childhood, Jasjit and I lived separately. My father spent a lot of his life in Europe, and because of slightly indifferent health, Jasjit also stayed with him. He went to 14 different schools. I stayed with my mother in India and went to nine different schools. We were separated by continents, and even a telephone call during those days was something of an impossibility. So Jasjit grew up with a largely absent mother and me with an absent father. We missed each other a lot. So after my father's demise, when we were reunited in India, there was a longing for togetherness. Importantly, my mother's great love and sacrifices have kept us together, even after she passed away.

On the demise of my father, we found that we had inherited a fledgling capsule company in debt. Perhaps a rare example of a start-up beginning with a negative cash and asset position.

As a small family of three, with responsibilities to revive and run a loss-making company at Kandivali, then a distant Mumbai suburb, my mother, Jasjit and I shifted to an apartment on top of the factory. Totally dedicated to the business, we slowly built up the company with a solid foundation. We learnt as we went along, without any mentor with industry experience to guide us. While working towards building up to something greater than us, our dependence on each other was nurtured to the extent that exists even today.

During all the years in Kandivali, we shared one office while handling separate areas of responsibility. The understanding of how each of us handled situations led to mutual appreciation and trust. We did disagree, even in the presence of managers, but that was always on business matters, never personal. We may not have always thought alike, but we respected each other's opinion. I always felt that if we both thought and acted alike, then one of us was redundant. Our different strengths, he an engineer and me with economics and marketing, were complementary. That gave great strength to the growing business. Both of us virtually were able to comprehend the other's experiences and thought process even before it was fully enunciated. And keep each other from "going over the top."

It was a very happy period of 20 years of living together, discussing over dinner what happened during the day and sharing our learning and enjoying our mother's amazing cooking.

As families grew, we worked together but started living separately instead of a joint family. This is another reason for the absence of family irritants that separate business families. Our wives also found their self-actualization in their relatively smaller businesses that we encouraged them to set up.

I think the initial struggles to save our business, to acquire technology and achieve a sustainable cash flow, helped keep us together. Working together to create something bigger than ourselves kept petty squabbles and irritations out of the way. It was gratifying to achieve many national and international awards and recognition. The expectation of reaching where hardly any Indian companies had been before, kept the excitement of business and our filial bonding alive.

Throughout our careers, there was no dishonesty. Neither with money or in our dealings with each other. The transparency cemented the relationship, and the clean and honest dealings with all also enabled us to sleep well at night and build up a reputation.

Between Jasjit and myself, the age difference is just 16 months. The succession from the last generation to ours and on to the next generation has been without any rancour or dispute. My nephew, Karan, who is now increasingly running the group, also has two young boys with almost exactly the same age difference. Looks like the Singhs will be around for some time!

We now employ over 5,000 personnel in 16 factories in India and overseas. We are professionally managed with excellent Indian and expat managers, and I hope that the close family relationship and caring with which we were brought up will continue across the group and future generations'.

And Martin Luther King when he said:

> 'Take the first step in faith. You don't have to see the whole staircase, just take the first step'.

A REVERSE SITUATION: THE DECLINE OF THE GUCCI FAMILY

It is not for nothing that Max Weber worked out that only 13% of family businesses survive through the third generation. The story of the Gucci family seems to prove this right. In the third generation, the Guccis' destroyed all that the grandfather and father had so assiduously built with caution, care, creativity and hard work.

Guccio Gucci started the company in Florence in the early days of the 20th century. He had started as a bellhop at the Savoy hotel in London, and saw that luggage and bags play a big role as status symbols for the rich and powerful. He did something about it rather than just observing this as a phenomenon. He went back to Italy, learned the leather trade, designed and marketed the GUCCI brand—stylish and expensive—and made it famous worldwide. Guccio was a classic case of an entrepreneur—he followed a dream and put it in action. When Guccio died in 1953, he left the business to his three sons (one son died soon after). The eldest Aldo ran the business and immediately set out to expand worldwide with stores in London, Tokyo, Paris and London. This was good, but the model he followed did cost a lot of money and cut into the profit. Yet Aldo kept Gucci stable and profitable during his reign.

When the third generation began to take an active interest in the business, troubles also began. Aldo's son, Paulo, wanted to create his own fashion line. The father and uncle Rodolfo (who had 50% share in the company) rebuffed the idea. He went ahead and launched it, and they cut off all ties with him. Paolo took revenge on his own father by exposing Aldo's tax issues, and Aldo had to serve one year in prison for tax evasion.

In 1983, after Aldo's brother Rodolfo died and his 50% share came to his son Maurizio, he teamed up with his cousin Paolo to run the business. Over time, their relationship soured, and once again Paolo reported Maurizio to the tax authorities. Maurizio had to flee to Switzerland. Paolo eventually launched his own fashion line which was a disaster. Maurizio ran the Gucci empire through the 1980s and brought it to a negative net worth of $17 million. He also had a personal debt of $40 million. He was forced out of the company by the majority stakeholder Investcorp. This stakeholder then took control and brought Gucci back to its pristine glory, without a Gucci to guide its destiny. In 1993, Maurizio was gunned down by the mafia in Milan, apparently on orders of his ex-wife. She was later sentenced to 29 years in jail for this crime. Thus, the end of the Gucci family—though not of the Gucci name! (*The Guardian* 2000).

Reflexion: Impact of the VUCA World

Most people who use the term VUCA world, may not be realizing the full impact of the short, very meaningful abbreviation. The full impact is felt only when you see a small machine, which in a few minutes of analyzing your skin, is able to tell you your age. This is the use of artificial intelligence (AI).

You feel the impact when you see someone in US, sitting in the office and being able to control all the machines in her home from the office—the IoT.

When you read the news item that in the third match and onwards of chess, the robot has beaten the human world champion—a feat that was thought improbable and impossible in the past. But it has now happened.

When you see a company like Tata, from a developing country like India, buying iconic product companies of the developed world, like Europe—Jaguar cars and Tetley Tea—you know it is a volatile world and complex.

Snapdeal, the online retail company had been boasting for some years that it was competing with Flipkart and would one day overtake the competitor. There was a show of strength with investments by eBay in Snapdeal. In this uncertain world, finally, Flipkart swallowed Snapdeal—and expanded its own horizons. In turn, it could tempt the two biggest e-commerce companies in the world to try to become its majority shareholders—Amazon and Walmart.

Finally, Walmart won to create a behemoth in the e-commerce world of India, where the original founders of Flipkart, Sachin and Binny Bansal, had 5.5% each of the shareholding! One of the founders had to leave with his booty of $1 billion into his first retirement at age 36. The press is busy with conjecture, that if Sachin Bansal were to put this money at low interest rate of 8% but with safe fixed deposits and pay the highest slab of 35.88% income tax, he will still get ₹10 million a day as income! In jest we would say, this seems to worry a lot of people who seem to know what they would do with this sum but don't have the money!

THE OUTCOME

The Flipkart–Walmart collaboration has created two camps of believers because of the ambiguity. One camp of believers thinks that such a deal is not good for Indian retailers and their growth will be impacted by a giant multinational with deep pockets. With the new competition, farmers and other vendors will be taken advantage of by the big buyer, and the consumer will gain only marginally with lower prices.

The other camp believes that it will be exactly the reverse. Because of a large movement in retail industry, markets will expand and create more jobs, more vendors, and the entire supply chain will be benefited. The argument used is that the retailer has not been wiped out even in the USA where Walmart is a major force.

The VUCA world has reduced a large number of jobs—replacement by automation. The highest use of automation in the world is in South Korea. Yet they seem to manage their employment rather well. Japan is also high in use of automation and has also managed to keep their population gainfully employed. The VUCA world will create issues which the family businesses will have to face, more and more in every generation, and the ability to provide good governance will determine whether the family business will continue to be successful.

Two perspectives; two conflicting viewpoints...only time will tell how the growth of the economy is impacted!

LOOKING AHEAD

In business as in life, there is no 'status quo'. You either move forward and onward, or you stay behind, then fall behind and die.

Growth, the second G the 5G success framework, is therefore a MUST.

Growth of family businesses is ensured by nurturing passionals who are also professionals.

By inculcating the growth mind-set, all those in the family and also in the business will have a common bond, and a common foundation of ethical values.

As a result of nature and nurture, if one is able to find some members in each generation who have the qualities of Agility and Absorption, plus fair judgement, and are leaders who are healthy, wealthy and wise, the family business will go on, for many generations until either there is degeneration or there are no successors anymore. There is a solution in the present time of a VUCA world where family businesses can professionalize their management and still be in charge and create wealth. Or can sell out the business for a fair and at times, even overvalued sums of money, and then ride into the sunset with the consolation that life is not eternal, for individuals or for enterprises!

3

GEN-NEXT

The Relay Race?

The ultimate test of man's conscience may be his willingness to sacrifice something today for future generations whose words of thanks will not be heard.

Gaylord Nelson

GEN-NEXT: THE THIRD G OF THE 5G SUCCESS FRAMEWORK

Since time immemorial, people seek a life that has a meaning. They want to matter and continue to exist by leaving a legacy for future generations. Whether an enterprise is built or wealth amassed or reputation gained, entrepreneurs desire immortality by leaving their business to Generation-Next (gen-next) so that after they are gone, they still exist in some way.

The involvement of families in businesses is very common, in India and across the globe—in Asia, Africa, Middle East, Latin America and in parts of Western Europe—though there is a lot of diversity. For example, according to Bertrand and Schoar (2006), 65% of the 20 largest firms in Argentina have at least a 20% family stake; in Hong Kong, this fraction is 70%. In contrast, in Japan, the fraction of family control among the 20 largest firms is only 5%. In India, almost 69% of the top 500 public listed companies in the Bombay Stock Exchange are family controlled (Dixit 2010).

Research reinforces participation and long-term commitment of families in their business. In the words of Giovanni Agnelli, the late patriarch of the Italian industrial dynasty and a principal shareholder of Fiat, 'The [family] company is an inheritance to be protected and handed on. It is the outcome of the next and each generation's commitment to the last' (Bertrand and Schoar 2006).

Developing gen-next and passing on the legacy is a vital element of the 5G success framework for family businesses, the other 4Gs being genesis, growth, governance and giving back.

REFORMS AND SOCIAL CULTURE

Prior to economic reforms in the 1990s, the Indian family structure was predominantly a joint family system. Traditionally, a joint family consists not only of the husband, wife and their children but also the grandchildren, uncles, aunties and cousins. Family rituals and customs are the mechanisms to keep multiple generations of siblings and cousins together, and to experience a sense of belongingness.

Since the globalization of economy, the VUCA winds of change have impacted business models as well as our socio-cultural fabric. We are witnessing the weakening of the joint family system with rise of smaller, nuclear families. The transition of leadership from the incumbent generation to gen-next was fairly structured as primogeniture succession. The eldest son (at times irrespective of capabilities) used to be the head of the business and the family. Succession happened by default rather than planning and considering long-term goals of the family business.

After a decade and a half in the 21st century, India's growth story is optimistic as one of the fastest growing emerging economy. Businesses have transformed, and have become more global and competitive. Yet succession largely remains an unplanned process. According to a PwC India family business survey report of 2016, 84% of family businesses expect to grow either steadily or aggressively by 2021. The concern is about the transition of leadership to the next generation. Almost 85% respondents are not prepared with a robust, documented succession plan! (Mathur 2016).

HOW THE BATONS ARE PASSED

How do family businesses deal with the gen-next? How do they pass on the legacy? Is there a method in madness?

Some families do it by familiarizing and involving children in the business from an early age, making them help out. Smaller businesses and smaller families are able to do this effectively. Working in the family business for gen-next becomes an instinctive choice. The motel industry in the USA managed by the Patel community from Gujarat is a shining example.

Others ensure that the children are suitably qualified to meet the professional needs of current times and can stand up to their future colleagues at work who are professional managers.

They are expected to be the family CEOs in the business.

Others ensure that the children work for other companies outside, and prove themselves before 'coming home!' The gen-next has to earn their way up.

Others insist that they start at the bottom of the ladder in their own company and work their way up. Though this process is hastened by the full knowledge that the scion is entitled to be the successor.

There are those children who still get the message 'you are trapped. You belong to the joint business family. Therefore you must align, or you have a lot to lose'.

AFTER PASSING THE BATON

There are members of gen-next who continue the legacy and carry the torch for another generation, taking it further and making it larger. India Inc. has innumerable examples, the recent ones being Mukesh Ambani, Kumar Mangalam Birla, Rajiv Bajaj and Nisaba Godrej.

Or there are members of second and third generations who have to face a VUCA world, both at the family and the business fronts. They may not have passion or resources to manage or may undermine values and governance in a fast-changing environment, like the Sarabhai family, once the doyens of textiles, or the Singh family, once a blue-chip Ranbaxy pharma.

Or the businesses have been taken over by investment companies or industry giants, such as AT&T buying out Time Warner, Microsoft acquiring LinkedIn, or Walmart acquiring Flipkart in the world's largest buyout deal of 2018.

Or the businesses have separated management from ownership, and oversee from a distance such as Merck Pharma or L'Oréal, but still retain majority ownership.

Or have now become 'minor partners' because the shareholding base is now so much larger. Although Cadbury continued as the single largest shareholder, it could not prevent a giant corporation like Kraft to buy up smaller shareholders and become the single largest shareholder—larger than Cadbury, and then proceed to buy up the Cadbury family stake in the company.

BUILDING LEGACY

It is the wish of each human being to live for long as if there is no end. But we know it cannot happen. There is an end—sooner or later. It is the same with a family business. We wish an eternal life to it, but it cannot be. The best way to deal with the mortality of a business is to plan in order to ensure that it can go on. Building a legacy is better in all sorts of things so that future generations don't have to reinvent the wheel. They can continue with whatever the former did and move forward.

Many founders express their desire to leave a legacy behind in the form of an enterprise they have created. They want their children to build larger empires on what they have created. However, in reality, they cannot leave behind the legacy by accident. It has to be planned. With intentions of building legacy, the founder-patriarchs can groom their children; they can create a culture of pride for the business among family members at home; they can be mentors to gen-next and prepare them to gradually take on the mantle, and can slip out with a hope that gen-next will do much better than they did.

Or they can take another route of building a legacy through non-family professionals. There are examples of Harsh Mariwala of Marico and Azim Premji of Wipro who inherited the companies and gave them a different direction with much bigger success.

On the other hand, there are many examples where the gen-next has sunk seemingly profitable companies. The recent ones being United Spirits and United Breweries in the second generation, and Gucci or Skol beer in their third and fourth generations.

In a VUCA environment, changes will be much faster. Successful, and even unsuccessful (but having potential), companies will be bought, sold, merged and made profitable. There are only two major requirements: first, it should be a product or service which is required by the customer who wants to purchase it; and second, the organization is capable of handling uncertainties and complexities swiftly.

Successful businesses will move from the founder to the family to succeeding generations. They may become corporations and public companies, which are then far removed from the founder. But with gen-next, the glory will be in the striving, never in the attaining.

Musings

I started the first marketing consulting firm in India in the early 1970s. My son did not want to carry on the business in spite of having academic qualifications to do so. He settled in Silicon Valley in USA and married an American of European origin, and now I find it difficult to understand my two teenage grandchildren who speak American when I speak English. They have gone beyond the millennial generation, into the next category of iGeneration, as it is known! This is how gaps increase between generations!

Walter Vieira

THE SURVIVAL CHALLENGE

Survival and longevity of family businesses is a topic close to the heart of all the business communities and also of great interest to researchers, advisors and media. Indian family firms that were earlier operating in a controlled economy are now exposed to the threats of globalization and digitalization. Challenges from the multinationals and international players are not only regarding management and technology but are also in terms of long-term viability of the business.

Newspaper headlines frequently talk about conflicts and splits in the family business. There have been almost 32 splits in large, prominent business houses in the last 50 years which have caught media attention. There may be more, not in the limelight. If families fail to balance their internal pressures and transform their business models swiftly, they will inevitably have to struggle for survival.

According to C.H. Unnikrishnan, many yesteryear champions such as the Birlas (excluding the A.V. Birla branch), the Nandas of Escorts, the Sarabhais and the Singhs of Ranbaxy have lost out either because of the division of the original empires or the next generation's inability to take the business forward. But many other remarkable old business families such as Tata, Kirloskar, Mahindra and Bajaj adopted professional management strategies much earlier, and grew by leaps and bounds (Unnikrishnan 2016).

PREPARING FOR SURVIVAL

A few sustain the winds of change, and many wither off. What is the success mantra for family businesses to continue to gen-next and their gen-next?

Family businesses consisting of two mutually independent ecosystems—family and business, have conflicting characteristics. Family is sensitive and emotional. Business is objective and rational. When the operating environment is under pressure, both the systems come under stress and develop their coping mechanism, and at times, fail to develop.

When families grow in size and generations, inter-personal communication among members suffers. It can lead to lack of transparency, followed by mistrust. Also, members have their own aspirations and personal agendas. Social influences of spouses, in-laws and friends also play a critical role. These are the triggers which impact core values laid by the founder-patriarch, resulting in a shortened life cycle of the family business.

In *The Living Company*, Aries de Geus (1997) studied Fortune 500 companies that had survived more than 100 years and came to the conclusions for their longevity as follows:

- Sensitivity to the environment allows the company to learn and adapt
- Cohesion and identity help the company build a community within itself
- Decentralized, autonomous units create new business relationships in different areas of activity
- Conservative financing assures growth and evolutionary development

The daunting challenge of survival for family business is to stay future-ready and sustain a culture of bonding. As Donnelly (1964) has stated, the balance between family and business interests is usually a psychological one, arising from the family's own personal sense of responsibility towards the business.

SUCCESSION CONUNDRUM: THE RULE OF 33/13/3

In India's growth story, continuity of family business has become a crucial agenda. Not because of growth opportunities but because of lack of succession planning. A PwC (2016) study mentions that 73% of the successors working for the business are in senior positions and about 34% are in junior or middle management. We can interpret that the older generation will have to plan for succession in few years and the junior successors will have to prepare for leadership positions.

In family businesses, there are more failures than long-term successes. Problems of succession lead to a high mortality rate of family businesses. Since the earlier estimates of Max Weber in the 1960s, many researchers have studied the life expectancy of family businesses. On an average, almost 67 businesses out of 100 new ones are either sold or split after the death or retirement of the founder. Only about 33 businesses survive to the second generation and last beyond 25 years. About 13 businesses migrate to a third generation with a life span of about 50–60 years. Only 3 or 4 businesses out of 100 continue to survive in the fourth generation (Dun & Bradstreet 1973), lasting beyond 75 years (see Figure 3.1).

FIGURE 3.1 33/13/3: THE LIFE SPAN OF A FAMILY BUSINESS

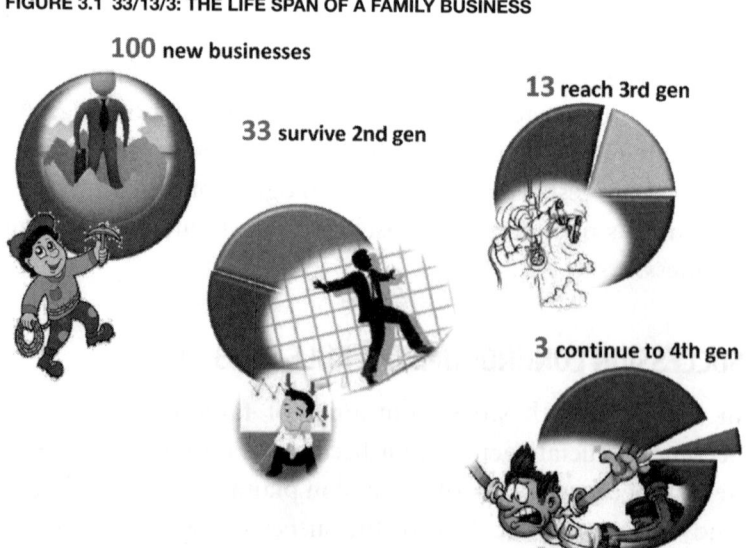

Source: Authors

CHANGING TREND OF SUCCESSION

One of the reasons of families caught off guard in the transition of leadership to the next generation is fast-changing social norm. The families are becoming nuclear with one or two children. In earlier times, it was not surprising to find eight or ten siblings. With shrinking families, there may not be children in the family to carry forward the business, or they may not be interested in the business for having a better career choice.

Millennial children born after 1980—who are privy to global education and transnational work culture—with their self-oriented approach towards life and independent thinking, may choose another career path if the family business does not appeal to them. Unlike their counterparts in the 1960s and 1970s, where working in the family business was not an option but was the sureshot way of life, for millennials, joining the business is not an obligation.

One more trend is impacting succession planning. The start-up bug with the gen-next is enticing and promising. Many gen-next scions of business families have opted to start their entrepreneurial journey (of course, the family is expected to be the angel investor!).

The absence of mentoring is one reason for the gen-next children to get disillusioned in the business and leave after working for a while. Professional training and grooming of gen-next is essential to prepare them for future leadership.

Some patriarchs deliberately defer the process of succession planning as their decisions could create conflict and criticism among the family. Some leaders find it difficult to let go of the reins and want to retain their powers as long as it is possible.

Also, issues like death could be a cultural issue and not openly discussed (Lamont 2010). Dhirubhai Ambani is known to have faced the dilemma of splitting the business between two successors while alive. After his death, acrimonious conflict between the brothers Mukesh and Anil became a global case study of conflict in family business.

Succession planning poses difficulties when some members work and some prefer not to work in the business. In such cases, families need to develop terms and conditions for inheritance and entitlement. Family's ownership interest, management responsibilities and policies of family's involvement in the business need to be defined as a part of governance.

ALL IN THE FAMILY

The Rothschild family is a case of dynastic thinking. The family began its ascent with Mayer Amschel Rothschild and pioneered international finance. That was the 18th century, and Europe was in a spree of industrialization. The Rothschilds made their fortune from exchange-rate transactions and bond-price speculation. They also developed the first international government bond market because of their close connections with governments throughout Europe. An essential part of Amschel Rothschild's strategy was to keep control of the business in family hands.

The Rothschild coat of arms was a clenched fist with five arrows symbolizing the five sons, with the family motto beneath: 'Concordia, Integritas, Industria' (Unity, Integrity, Diligence). In his will, Amschel set the rules that would closely tie his family to the future of the business he had started. In particular, he dictated that all key positions in the House of Rothschild were to be held by male members of the family and that the family was to intermarry with their own first or second cousins. Such rules created a long-term commitment of the Rothschild family to the banking business. In 2018, the Rothschild banking dynasty was passed on to the seventh generation.

In 'The Role of Family in Family Firms', Bertrand and Schoar (2006) studied Indian family businesses as a part of the global sample. They found that in India family norms are fairly stable over the short to medium run, even in rapid growth environments and possibly across generations. A main reason for the long-term stability of the family and leadership is a positive correlation between trust and values of the family. As generations progress, values tend to dilute because of various forces. Indian culture, religious ethos and family values promote congeniality and trust among family members. On similar lines, Jim Walton of Walmart describes his family's perspective on their involvement with Walmart, 'we view [the company] really more as a legacy we are responsible for, rather than something we own'.

WHEN THE NAME CASTS A SHADOW!

In a family business, the shadow of the founder falls across the whole organization, however large the organization may be. This is not just when the founder is alive but can also be across generations. Corporate lore is developed and becomes a part of corporate history. The family name is recognized for generations as we have seen with the Rockefellers, Fords, Hilton, Agnelli, Cadbury, Merck, Tata, Birla and many others. It is especially so when the last name of the founder is also the name of the company.

For better or for worse, carrying the last name is a heavy burden, especially if one is caught doing something that is disapproved by the family, or the community or the business fraternity. Such a burden has been carried by someone like Paris Hilton.

She is always under the glare of media headlights on her personal and social life. Of course, Paris has trodden her path without being constrained by the media and the burden of the surname. She could not be browbeaten into being a conformist for the sake of her family. Finally, the father had to go public and break the family connection with her to save the family any further embarrassment. But it did not matter to Paris, and she continued on her chosen path regardless, with the last name of Hilton still attached to her, and the perceived damage to the Hilton name continued.

There is something about the legacy that human beings expect and respect—and they do so even if there has been a break. Sometimes, it is also a help to separate out the name of the company from the name of the founder. In the case of great mismanagement or great frauds, the company can go on, without the stigma of the founder's name being attached for generations.

Satyam Computers, once a blue-chip company owned by Ramalinga Raju, met with a sudden fall because of the greed of the owner and unethical practices. Ranbaxy Laboratories, a pharmaceutical icon, was sold by the third generation Singh brothers—and later got caught in controversy of lack of governance in business dealings. Many other companies have had problems, and many have even come to a sorry end. But such companies do not bear the burden of the founder name. They can find a new 'avatar' under gen-next, and guide the management and go on for the benefit of the employees, the customer and the community.

WHEN THE NAME SHINES

Most humans are hero worshippers. They have been in awe of kings in the past, and then they have been in awe of the kings of commerce when commerce became so large that sometimes it exceeded the wealth of kings! There has been awe for the name of Tatas—starting with Jamshedji Tata, to Sir Dorab and to J.R.D. Tata, and then in a more democratic environment, to Ratan Tata. They have all tried to live up to the Tata name for over a century—until just now, when there is no longer a Tata at the head of one of India's largest conglomerates.

There is another legacy we respect and admire—that of G.D. Birla, the founder of the Birla empire. It was said that G.D. Birla used to keep 'real-time' data, an everyday record of performance of each of his major companies—sales, production, collection and outstanding. No one could pull the wool over his eyes. And in addition, he had people skills that few can imitate, even his progeny. He had the ability to know by name most of the managers in his companies and often even the names of their wives. He took an interest in the progress of studies of their children and their health. Though the number of employees in those days was less, but it is a quality to be admired.

In today's large corporates, the easier route is to surround oneself with a coterie of Richelieu (private advisors), so that the general interaction is minimal. If the sales and profits of the companies continue to be positive, there is no urgent need for the human touch of the G.D. Birla variety!

Musings

The stories of the Tatas are many, and there are books written about them. One hears of Jamshedji Tata taking friends on picnics to Khandala, the hills near Mumbai, and telling them that in Switzerland they convert the waterfalls into electricity and we should do this here sometime. And he did. That is how Tata Power was born! And when the villages around objected to the project, Jamshedji was practical and generous enough to negotiate, overcome their fears and give them free power for a limited number of years as a bargained settlement. But he did not let Tata Power abort. True story? Likely. But also lore!

Similarly, Sir Adrian Cadbury was known to be committed, highly ethical and efficient. He continued the legacy of building a large business enterprise that began four generations ago by the founder John Cadbury. Not only did the Cadbury family build a highly successful business, they also provided employment to a whole township of people near Birmingham and set up many institutions for their welfare. Sir Adrian Cadbury was appointed by the UK government to head the Committee on Corporate Governance. He became a respected man in the UK and even worldwide. All the members of the family wore the Cadbury name with pride.

THE CHALLENGE OF INHERITING 'POWER-ABILITY'

The entrepreneur who starts and grows the business has learnt through the school of experience how to acquire, manage and cultivate power. This power is then used to manage the business in its cycles of growth, consolidation and further growth.

However, successors acquire power by their lineage. They are 'born powerful'. They know, and others know that it is their entitlement. They are born with rights and, unfortunately, sometimes forget that they are also born with 'obligations'.

When Henry Ford checked into the Waldorf Astoria Hotel in New York late one evening, having missed the last flight to Detroit, he was immediately taken to the Presidential suite.

He complained because he had just wanted a single room for the night as he was leaving early the next morning. 'Your son always stays here when he is in New York', said the General Manager to Mr Henry Ford. Quick came the response, 'My son has a rich father, I don't!'

However, it is not easy for children to remember that they have also inherited an obligation, beyond the power and wealth. Daniel Vasella, Chairman of Novartis, described the concept of leadership aesthetically and very simply. When he was with a vineyard owner, the owner pointed to a stone wall and explained how his grandfather had started building it, then his father added to it and so did he. Whether great monuments or great businesses, they are not built in one generation.

There are several implications of this reality for gen-next inheritors in the family business. First, they are not in the business just to take advantage but to add. Second, it is crucial that the overall vision is shared by several people—both family and professionals. Beyond the first generation, it is difficult to understand and imbibe these implications. Pelf and power are taken as a right when one is born in a golden cage.

Some entrepreneurs try and correct the inbuilt failing by getting their children to begin careers on the factory floor.

To an extent, it does help. But the co-workers know that children will be rapidly moved up. Earning respect from co-workers and gaining their support by merit rather than the family name is a challenge for gen-next, which they must face and win over.

Other entrepreneurs will ensure that their children work for some other company for experience for several years before doors are opened to the parental company. They can then demonstrate that they have earned spurs in a 'neutral' environment and therefore they deserve a place at the 'high table'.

It is said that some achieve greatness, others strive for greatness. Still others have greatness thrust on them. It is the same with power. Those in the succeeding generations, generally belong to the third category where the family label is thrust on them. And if they are sincere and disciplined, they can move to the second and then to the first category of achieving greatness.

THE CASE OF ENTITLEMENT: MASKED BEHIND TITLES

It would seem that titles are always important. They are more important when they are inherited. At least they seem to be. Haile Selassie of Ethiopia (late lamented) described himself as the Emperor of Ethiopia, Lion of Judah, Descendant of Solomon and Sheba, and much else. The titles of present-day Emperors of Japan and Thailand also run into many lines!

In the business world, there is a limit to how and where the titles can be used or NOT used.

In one of the largest family-controlled, public listed companies in India—Cipla—the management decided to discontinue all titles. The visiting card just showed the name, department and company name. Many executives quit and joined other companies. They felt 'orphaned' without a title. Many others stayed on, albeit reluctantly, and finally got used to it. Cipla was a titleless organization for over ten years and yet grew to become one among the top three pharmaceuticals companies in India. With changing times, Cipla reinstated titles and now follows the normal business practice.

At the other extreme are banks, especially multinational banks who distribute titles of vice president liberally and generously. Such a practice helps to give even junior executives an entry to meeting with senior decision-makers in client companies. Otherwise, they would not even get a chance to make an initial presentation. It is the same with airlines, and insurance and finance companies. They need an entry, and they use the title as a 'bait'.

In the family business, are titles important to the founder or the founder's children or grandchildren? Is the last name itself not sufficient and self-proclaiming? Do the Rockefellers, Fords, Pierre Cardin and Gates have to establish their positions by describing themselves as President or CEO or any other title?

A part of the answer was found from a third-generation family company where 14 grandchildren were employed in the worldwide operations as presidents and vice presidents in different locations. Many of them were not pulling their weight. A senior consultant was given the task to assess their suitability for the present position and report to the chairman who was also the head of the family. The consultant found eight of them unsuitable for the position and also lacking in skills for any commercial activity. They had neither the education nor the experience or the ability to learn. They were a 'drag' on the performance of the group.

After the assessment, the consultant got these eight family members to agree to resign from their assignment and be free to continue with whatever their hobby or passion was—art, golf, or just travel. They would be paid all the emoluments and benefits they were getting then and would get substantial dividends on their shareholding. All of them agreed to sign an undertaking, and the consultant was pleased that the project was successful. The Chairman was even more pleased that 'operation weeding out' was complete without ill feeling or rancour!

A fortnight later, the consultant began to receive notes from each of them withdrawing from the agreement. What had happened? The wives of all eight had objected that their husbands cannot quit their jobs. What will people say? Can they answer the question 'what does your husband do', by saying 'Nothing. He plays golf. He paints'. They can no longer say, he is president of X Corporation. The wives needed a title for their husbands, even more than the husbands did. The title was an anchor in the social circle they moved in.

Titles are important even when the last name commands easy recognition in a family business. Even if the title is Special Assistant to the Chairman, and even if the special assistant is the chairman's son!

WOMEN IN FAMILY BUSINESS

Although we have progressed greatly in the 21st century, in India and in much of other parts of the world, women are not seen playing a visible role in their family businesses. 'Visible role' is the right description because it is usually the man who is the founder. In the early growth stage, it is the wife who provides the support which enables the husband to move ahead in the sometimes choppy seas of business. Without that kind of support, the business might not progress so fast or so well. Times have changed and women are as enterprising as men, though much less in numbers.

During the 1920s, an unusual businesswoman, Sumati Morarjee, became an icon for women in family business. She ran the Scindia Steamship Company (one of the blue chips at that time). She ran it effectively, efficiently and sometimes with an iron hand. In social context, it was a courageous step for a woman in a conservative male-dominated society to take over the family's running business after her husband died in his 50s. And she did so with aplomb to win kudos from all around!

More recently, there was the case of Rohinton D. Aga who was a son-in-law of A.S. Bathena, and the successor of Themax, an energy company in Pune, India. He grew Thermax to a mid-sized company and then a public listed company. When he suddenly died, his wife Anu Aga took over the leadership without any experience of the corporate world. She took the company much ahead with the help of her professional team of managers.

In India, many use the phrase, 'I got my daughter married off', implying that they have done their duty as parents, and now it is the duty of the husband and his family to look after her. She no longer has much to do with father's family or his business. Thermax family of Aga and Pudumjee are an exception! Anu Aga has passed on the baton to her daughter Meher Pudumjee who is now leading the business along with her husband Pheroz Pudumjee as the non-executive director. Pheroz recalls a lesson passed on to him by his father-in-law R.D. Aga: 'Profits are not just a set of figures, but a set of values'.

Ninfa in San Francisco took charge of the Shangri-La Motel after her husband died suddenly. She diversified into launderettes and apartment leasing business, and quit the more arduous motel business—and in turn trained her two children to assist her and then take over new businesses.

There is the case of the Ambani brothers and the siblings' feud that followed after the death of the father Dhirubhai Ambani, the founder of Reliance Group, one of India's top three businesses. The brothers were at loggerheads with considerable dissonance. Millions of shareholders were worried about the future of this large group until the mother, Kokilaben, stepped in to settle the dispute and ensured that the warring factions made peace. She was a woman who seldom shared the stage with her high profile husband Dhirubhai in the past, though she had been his major support in the background. She knew enough. And she could use reason, persuasion, affection and love to manage a complicated situation where the founder of India's largest business empire had died inexplicably without a leaving a will!

There are those like Ms Lillien Bettencourt, heiress of L'Oréal, who at some point opted out of operations and left it to professionals to manage the company. And they do this so efficiently and well that Ms Bettencourt was world's richest woman when she died in 2017 at an age of 94.

Women from business families, though not actively participating in the business, are a critical part of the organization. They may sometimes be invisible and beyond the camera glare, managing family dynamics as the CEO—chief emotional officer. Sometimes, they may be alongside, but a few steps behind. And very occasionally, ahead, leading the family and business. But they are there—an integral part of family business.

FOR THE SAKE OF THE CHILDREN

We do know the great corporations of the past were built from generation to generation. But in changed times, the succession concept is also changing. There are business families today where the founders do not want to leave a legacy to their children. They want the children to begin at the beginning and taste success or failure as the case may be. All that the progeny may inherit is the last name—for all that it may be worth! There are self-made millionaires and billionaires across various fields, from rock stars to mayors, who want their children to have as normal a childhood as possible so that they learn the value of money, and build their careers and their fortunes.

There is Bill Gates, America's richest man, who has directed his $90 billion fortune to his foundation for charity. He has said in the past that his children won't be billionaires as he is giving so much money away.

There is Warren Buffett, with $63 billion in wealth, who has already pledged away 99% of his fortune, and a lot of it to the Bill and Melinda Gates Foundation. He has stated that, 'he would provide for his kids just enough so that they can do anything; but not so much that they feel like doing nothing'.[1]

There is Michael Bloomberg, politician and entrepreneur, with $34 billion—nearly all of which will go to non-profit organizations and charities across the globe. None of it will go to his children or family members. He says that the best financial planning ends with bouncing the cheque to the undertaker. Refrains of the old song—*you can't take it with you!*

---

[1]See http://fortune.com/2012/11/21/should-you-leave-it-all-to-the-children/, accessed 19 June 2018.

It is the same with music composer Andrew Llyod Webber with $1.2 billion who will use his wealth to discover and nourish fresh talent—to encourage the arts, rather than raise brats. Or George Lucas, the film director of *Star Wars* with $5.2 billion, who has warned his children that their inheritance will be meagre. Or Ted Turner, the media tycoon with $2.2 billion, who has already channelled millions to the UN Foundation and many more charities—and the only money left for his family of five children will be for his funeral expenses.

Will billionaire families in the East be influenced by this new trend in the West? In an environment where beyond business even elected political office is considered inheritance and entitlement for the next generation, it may not be fertile ground for such new ideas. At least, not yet!

GUIDING CHILDREN TO FOLLOW THEIR STAR

Ivan Fernandes was awarded the Dubai Entrepreneur of the Year Award in 2009. He is the innovator and serial entrepreneur who developed many technologies, the most significant being RTGS—real time gross settlement. The technology enabled bank-to-bank money transferred real time, throughout the world, and changed the face of financial transactions everywhere.

Ivan had humble beginnings and in a career spanning India, Saudi Arabia and UAE. He has built the successful and innovative Ducont Company in Dubai. Ivan is also a mentor to some young entrepreneurs who are in the 'struggle situation' on the entrepreneurial roadway.

Between the two extremes of leaving the whole fortune to inheritors and leaving just enough are people like Ivan, who has encouraged his 10-year-old son to work towards being a professional golfer! His son showed great promise on the golf course at a tender age and he was also passionate about the sport. So Ivan sent him to Florida in the USA at age 10 to a training school for young athletes. He and his wife support and accompany their son on the golf tournament circuit.

Ivan, the software entrepreneur, is fanning the flame of his son's passion by putting in substantial amount of time and money rather than channelling his son's ambitions into expanding the Ducont Company. He is helping his son to follow his star!

There is a parallel with Leander Paes among the stars of the tennis world. Dr Vincy Paes, a medical practitioner, encouraged his son who showed promise of being a professional tennis player, and financed his training in the USA at considerable sacrifice. Finally, he even gave up medical practice to accompany his son on the tournament circuit. Did Dr Vincy want his son to be a doctor and follow in his footsteps? In the early years, sure he did. But Leander followed a different beat to the sound of a different drum. His father, a professional like entrepreneur Ivan, let him be.

FAMILY TIME FOR FAMILY BONDING: HELPS TO CARRY THE TORCH

How does succession work in family business? What is the right thing to do? Each family has to work out its own solution.

When a family business starts and is on the way to being established, for the entrepreneur, it seems much easier to spend family time during business time and work on business during family time. It is because, family and business activities are intertwined and overlap. Unintended, but happening nevertheless!

Joe, of Indian origin and working in Kenya, emigrated to California in the 1970s and started the Shangrila motel in San Francisco. His wife helped him with all the housekeeping that needed to be done. The teenage son and daughter helped the parents after their school time. Part of the evenings were spent together, doing school homework and dining together. After a while, the mother started a few launderettes and the boy gave a helping hand every other day. When Joe died rather prematurely, the son and daughter moved on with the business under the titular leadership of the mother. They also diversified in another business of buying and renting apartments. The parents had guided the children through school and in business—and all the transitions were as smooth and as painless as could be.

The third-generation patriarch of S.K. Pharmaceuticals in Mumbai, late Jayantilal Shah, guided a family of about 100 members, and businesses with 13 cousins and nephews until he retired at the age of 75. The 85-year-old family business has grown and expanded into multiple areas in the pharmaceutical industry. All the male members of the 3rd and 4th generations work the business by their own choice. The family has never experienced a conflict or split in the business.

Since 1978, the S.K. family follows a protocol, the family's annual vacation. During Diwali festival, the entire family of 100+, including siblings, cousins and nephews with their families, spend four days together. Family vacation is a common practice in many families, but in S.K. family, it is unique. Fun and learning are combined. Gen-next members are given responsibilities to plan and implement the entire event under the guidance of seniors. Lessons of leadership, team building, communication and inclusiveness are learned while having fun. Family stories are told and shared, which is an important aspect of family bonding. Each generation has its own set of experiences, but the power of stories about past experiences often have a deep impression on the gen-next members (Cohen and Sharma 2016).

Such a ritual helps bonding and creating understanding, and building bridges for relationship among members and spouses of varied generations. Jayantilal Shah used to say, 'the family that prays and plays together, stays together'. Indeed, a way to pass on the torch to gen-next!

BRIDGING THE SUCCESSION GAP

As the business grows, the entrepreneur gets busier and also richer. Children are sent to fashionable boarding schools, and perhaps the family meets twice a year at holiday time—and that is all the connection! In all likelihood, the emotional connect and bonding among parents and children becomes weak. When children leave and do not want to join the family business as wished by parents, the entire lesson of 'building the legacy' has gone haywire!

In some family businesses, parents do manage to let children go and yet keep them in. A look at the 10 wealthiest business families in India shows that all their children after studying abroad, came back to the business. There are the Birlas, Jindal, Nader, Mahindra, Ambani, Thapar and many others. It is likely that these businesses were already grown so large that the options available outside to the gen-next paled in comparison to what was available to them at home.

Even greater credit must be given to those who came back to much smaller family business empires to initiate a change in direction and take the company to astounding heights. Azim

Premji did it with Wipro and took it from hydrogenated oils to IT, hardware and software. Jasjit and Ajit Singh did this with Associated Capsules to make it among the largest in the world in hard gelatin capsules. In spite of geographic distance, when their father died, they heard the call and joined business, like the Roman farmer who heard that Rome was under attack, lay down the plough and took up arms to defend the city.

Around the world, family businesses have tried to find solutions to their legacy problems.

In Japan, the practice is to pass on the business to the eldest son so that the legacy continues without splits or disruption due to conflict of siblings. Many a time, a son or son-in-law is adopted to continue the lineage as successors.

Others have had 'in-laws' inducted into the business and have also found that it works. Still, others have moved away from operations and hired well-paid professional managers to run the show. They only get involved with strategy and governance.

Many others now, such as GMR, TVS group and Chanrai group, have a family trust or a family office, and are largely concerned with managing wealth and maintaining values of the company. This seems to work best with all family members getting a piece of the cake and yet being free to pursue their interests.

CONTINUITY: A CONSCIOUS EFFORT

Continuity of family business is a daunting challenge, even though it may be every entrepreneur's wish. At best, by the third generation, the successors lose interest in the business as environment changes and the business model may not be lucrative or may be very competitive. Or the successor may not have competencies or lose the ability to work as hard as required. The flame of entrepreneurship gets dampened. Unless the family takes conscious steps to keep gen-next interested and prepare them to keep the flame alive, the company goes into a decline.

Such is the fate of Stroh beer company, founded 149 years ago by a German immigrant in Detroit. He built it into one of the largest beer companies in the USA. The fourth generation successor felt he was imprisoned in the job in his company. He wanted to be a professional photographer. The worst part was, he lived a lavish lifestyle—so money was flowing out much faster than money flowing in. Finally, Stroh was declared bankrupt, and he had to move into a home for the aged. A sad end to a glorious history of nearly 150 years, a legacy short-lived!

FIRM BORDERS BECOME POROUS OVER TIME

There are no clear lines drawn in the involvement of the family and the business in the initial stages of setting up an enterprise. Often, everyone in the family is engaged in one way or another while the head of the family tries to make headway. As the business grows, organization expands and generations are added, and the partitions begin to form. These are invisible at first and barely visible even later on. To an outsider, it takes a long time to recognize these rifts. The insider-outsider, like an in-law, may help to identify cracks with an unbiased perspective. Total outsiders may perhaps never recognize the undercurrents or may take a long time.

There is the case of the owner of a hotel chain in North India who had started with just one hotel but grew the empire over a period. He needed efficient and confidential help.

His son-in-law proved to be an ideal fit. He worked with his 'papa' for some decades until the owner's sons grew up and joined the business. The sons felt that they had the right of way.

They felt that the brother-in-law was an outsider who had gained the trust of the father. They made it difficult for the brother-in-law till he quit to do something else in life. Fortunately, the sons did well and prospered. Even though son-in-law belonged to the family, he was only an in-law!

Jay was an exceptionally bright young man. With an engineering degree from IIT (Indian Institute of Technology) followed by an MBA from IIM (Indian Institute of Management), he had the key that opens doors everywhere. He then joined a multinational and had an exceptionally successful career. His climb on the corporate ladder was as expected, steady without much conflict. However, when it came to the last phase—the promotion to MD's position—another colleague beat him to the finishing line. The company felt they needed someone strong in finance as the new MD and Jay was not. Jay had to be content to be number two.

He continued in the company, but he now was taking orders from a former colleague who was also a few years junior in age. Such instances happen all the time in the corporate world, but that was small consolation. A few years later, Jay was invited to join a large family-controlled group as vice-chairman, and since the present chairman was nearly 70 years old, Jay thought that maybe he will still be a chairman at the end of his career. Alas! This was not to be.

The chairman found a successor from his community and distantly related. The belief that a distant relative is preferable to a rank outsider. Another opportunity had passed by for Jay who was fated to end his career as a vice-chairman.

Very often, one discovers that in organizations which are family-run, blood is thicker than outsiders. One has to take cognizance of these affiliations.

GHOSTS FROM THE FUTURE

When the story blew up in the Indian media of how the four grandchildren of Vijaypat Singhania of Raymonds, one of India's tycoons of the textile industry, filed a court case against the grandfather asking for a better and bigger share of the family fortunes, it was like a ghost from the future. Most of us are familiar with ghosts from the past, but this one was different.

Although the baron, Singhania, had already settled inheritance with the older son many years ago and had appointed the younger son to take over and run the company, the grandchildren, who had now come of age, felt that their father had been short-changed. Now they claimed their (or father's) rightful share. Is it right to resurrect the past? Only a court decision will tell. It was a ghost from the future!

The daughter of Niranjan Hiranandani, a prominent builder in Mumbai, India had married and settled in the UK. She got into a new venture with the support of her father. The company ran into some significant losses, and the daughter blamed her father for not providing the amount of money promised as an investment. She filed a court case for losses and damages. The father said it is a case of misunderstanding. The daughter's position is different. The battle goes on. Ghosts from the future!

Dr Costa, a technical genius, founded the largest table wine and canned food company in Goa, India. He took his cousin and a close friend Bill as a junior partner. Bill was young and did not have any special skills to contribute to the company, and he looked after administration and melange activities. Costa did not mind this—and he was just happy that Bill was around.

All went well for 30 years until the sons of both the partners grew up into their 20s and joined the company. They were both cast in their respective fathers' moulds, But the Costa heir was not prepared to be as tolerant as his father had been. Things came to a head when both the heirs had a heated argument in the office one evening and came to blows—much to the chagrin of all the office staff. The two senior partners were ashamed and embarrassed. Costa decided to buy up the shares of the minor partner and called a mutually acceptable mediator to broker the deal.

Thus ended a 30-year partnership between cousins and between friends. The next generation had taken over. In spite of fairness in the final deal and the separation, there was a trail of bitterness. Ghosts from the future had given a new direction to the fortunes of an otherwise successful family enterprise.

IN FAMILY SUCCESSION, MAN PROPOSES...

In some families, when all seems to be perfectly planned and going smoothly, there can be a hiccup, or there can be a cough or worse! It is best to adopt an attitude that 'if things CAN go wrong, they WILL'—the wisdom of Murphy.

Such an instance happened with the British royal family. There was Edward, Prince of Wales, young and handsome, the successor to the throne and the darling of the nation. He was even the chief host, receiving and entertaining foreign royalty, and accepted as the heir to the throne, succeeding his father, King George V. From his childhood he was 'trained for kingship'. But it was not to be. Edward fell in love with an American socialite and gave up his claim to the throne for the love of his life! George VI, his younger brother, was pushed into being the heir. He spoke with a stammer which got accentuated with public speaking, and his walk showed lack of confidence. He missed out on the 'training for kingship', and yet he became the king and remained so for a long time.

There was the scion of a large textile conglomerate in India, who was the firstborn and identified as the 'son and heir apparent', and was trained by the father and other senior managers to take charge when the time came. Somewhere along the way, the young man became an alcoholic and could neither take care of his family nor his business. All attempts to cure him failed. The younger son, who was untrained for such a responsible position, and for whom spirituality was more important than business, was forced into the 'successor' slot. He meandered through his term, reluctantly but adequately, for many years. For him, it was a 'burdensome yoke' for the sake of the family. Eventually the business went into a decline.

Joseph Kennedy, the millionaire businessman in Boston, wanted to achieve 'family power' since he had acquired 'family wealth'. He placed his bets on his eldest son, Joseph, and facilitated in whatever way he could to put Joseph in line to be elected president of the USA. This was not to be. Joseph died during the war when he was in the armed forces. Joseph Sr. was devastated but not helpless. He changed his focus to the next in line—John. John F. Kennedy became President of the USA, and will perhaps be remembered as among the most outstanding presidents of the USA in recent history.

There are different ways of facing a situation where 'man proposes, and God disposes'.

The last resort is to sell out the business completely in the absence of an heir, as some do. Others try to find solutions which may not be as good or are sometimes better than the initially planned solution. In the VUCA world, a preferred solution is to professionalize the business and allow competent outsiders to manage the business.

Handing Over the Baton

Harish Mehta, CMD, Onward Technologies Ltd shared his views and experience on transferring leadership to the gen-next successor.

'My son (Jigar) had been working with me in the company for over ten years. He knew the business well, and was aware of the present status and the future possibilities. Having your eyes on the future is always important but even more so when you are in the information technology business. Because in this business, the future could literally be tomorrow!

Jigar also had his own ideas of how our business should take shape going forward. Some good ideas, and some that did not excite me as much. I am surprised that in that long period of 10 years he did not get completely frustrated and walked off.

Two years back, I moved on to become a chairman of the company and the board of directors selected my son as managing director of the company. Our engineering business was expanding in Pune, and seeing huge potential in the business globally, he moved to Pune to be close to the action, while I stayed in Mumbai. I became the absentee landlord. The figurehead you hear of but seldom interact with. It also established to me that the company could do without me and therefore I will not be missed when I "slip out".

I would say I have been lucky, unlike many other family businesses that I know, that I had a successor with both the attitude and the aptitude to take over the business. I knew that he had the same love and affection for the company as I had. That he had the patience to wait to take the corner office, even when I had delayed it by a couple of years with a false dependence on my own indispensability. I was even more fortunate that we expanded to a new location which made the transition even smoother, completely organic and relatively easier than it otherwise could have been.

Onward Technologies and I, have indeed been blessed. Succession planning never became the big challenge that books on family business write about!'

HOW LONG DO LEGACIES LAST?

There are reports of companies in Europe that have been in the care of the founding families for seven, eight and, in one case, sixteen generations! This comes as a pleasant surprise. We are all used to seeing the dynasty dying out after the third generation, or the fourth, to the maximum. Then, they disappear, and all that is left behind is the name.

In this millennium age, with the tech start-ups that we see every month and with the founders in their 20s, some of whom become billionaires in their 30s, few think about succession. Their focus is on how they can cash out of the new enterprise they have started and move on to the next project. These serial entrepreneurs produce projects rather than progeny!

In many of the start-ups, which sometimes grow into massive enterprises (and need venture capital to enable them to do this), the founders then become minor shareholders. They may still remain the single largest shareholders, but they can be voted out. This is not a situation which helps to promote family business. There is no legacy. Only a partial ownership in a company without any major say in the management. So the founders like Bill Gates have opted out and gone away to do something else ensuring that Microsoft will be managed by professionals who have skills to carry the enterprise forward.

There are others like Yadav of Housing.com in India who was asked to quit as CEO even before he got started by the majority of the shareholders. And there is the founder of Uber who was virtually forced to resign, just as the company was making the great push forward.

In any case, these two options are better than the history of one of the big leather goods manufacturers of India. The family built a large business with five factories in South India and large exports to Europe and the USA. When the chairman died suddenly, the son-in-law Sunil was to take over. He was a leather technologist who worked for the company for eight years and was being groomed as the successor, on the recommendation of the management consultants to the company.

Sunil was both qualified and had the experience having worked long enough in the company. But events took a different turn. After the funeral rites were over, the mother took a lead role in decision-making. She insisted that the chairmanship should go to the son and not to the son-in-law. She prevailed on the son not to return to the USA, but to stay back and take over the reins of the company. The son was a medical doctor and worked for a pharmaceutical company in New York. He did not have a clue about the leather industry.

Instead of saying a firm NO, he stayed back and inherited the title of executive chairman.

The son-in-law quietly left to start his own business in leather trading. It took less than three years for the whole empire to fold up. Most of the properties were sold to pay debts. A glorious run of 39 years had come to a sorry and abrupt end.

Japan has managed to have several of world's oldest businesses. The oldest family business, Kongo Gumi in the business of building temples, lasted for about 1,400 years and 38 generations. Eventually, not able to withstand VUCA forces, the business went bankrupt and was taken over by a construction business group. In such exceptionally long generational continuity, many times the family has to adopt a child. The child takes on the family name and the inheritance, and is trained to 'continue building the garden wall', a process started by his predecessors. The disadvantage of softness developed over generations of success and the good life do not show up in the 'adopted heir'. Is that the answer to those in other parts of the world? Who knows!

SUCCESSION PLANNING: DIFFERENT VIEWS IN THE EAST AND THE WEST

Until a few years ago, we did not realize that there were different views on succession planning in family businesses in the East and the West. We are all products of our environment. In the East, we start a business and grow it so that it is there for our succeeding generations and hopefully for many generations! It may or may not happen, but at least it is a dream.

We hope that future generations will have the same passion and commitment as their seniors to start the business, and they will continue to grow it on the foundations which the founder has laid. There is also the hope that they will improve on what has been done, and the name we have established will be known, admired and respected for generations to come—like in the case of Cardin and Canali, Ford and Boehringer, and Tata and Birla. From this attitude, is derived the yearning for a male child in every generation who will carry the 'name' forward with pride and satisfaction. In essence, in the East, we feel compelled to build our legacy for our descendants.

In the West, the culture is different. Entrepreneurs build companies for their satisfaction, for a feeling of self-fulfilment, for a feeling of achievement and to do what they have a passion for. And having built a company, big or small—and having proved to themselves that they can do it—they may one day decide to sell the company they have created, hang up their boots and retire to exotic vacation places. The children will get an inheritance of wealth, but may not necessarily inherit the company and participate in its operations!

Reflexion: East and West

I was on a trans-atlantic flight from Lisbon to New York, when I began a conversation with my co-passenger. He was a friendly person and disclosed that he was the owner of a large ship repair company in Vancouver. He had gone with a team to deal with a problem with a client ship, now docked in Italy. Having attended to it, he was now heading back—leaving his team to deal with the details of the operations.

We then got talking about how he had started the company 35 years ago and how he had toiled to build it into the sizable company it now was. And now he was 76 and wanted to retire and just take it easy. 'Are your children in the business?'

I asked him. 'Yes', he said. 'One of my two sons, John, has been working in the business for the last six years. He has shaped up well. The other son is a journalist and does not want to be a part of what I do, which is just as well'.

'So you are lucky to have John take over', I ventured. He was silent for some time.

'Let's see. I have asked him to pay me the market valuation of the company less 20% and pay it in four equal annual instalments—since he is my son. If he can, then the company is his. If he can't then I have other offers and I will sell. I cannot make it any easier for my son. I do not want to give it to him free and on a platter, because he will never know or understand the value and the sacrifices I have made to bring it to this level. And then, he will ruin it!'

I thought about this rational, logical submission by the owner of a family business in the West—and juxtaposed it with the emotional, familial attitudes in the East. Each approaching the same dilemma in their own style and in their own way. And there can be no judgement, because we are all products of nature and nurture—where we were born and how we have been brought up!

Walter Vieira

PREPARING THE GEN-NEXT

Is there any formula for preparing the gen-next to take over the reins of business successfully?

Preparing the gen-next for succession can be a joyous ride or can be a nightmare for families, depending on their consciousness and quality of preparation. A successor groomed from a young age would be more involved and passionate about the business than a successor joining the business as a career option. Instead of ownership and management control, both with the family, now the businesses are moving towards ownership control with the family and management control with professionals. What can be a better option than to develop professional successors from the family itself?

From our research and experience, we have identified three keys for an effective succession planning for business families aspiring to handover the baton to gen-next (Dixit 2015).

Start Early

Childhood impressions are lifelong impressions. If children are exposed to the business environment, and a sense of pride for the business is cultivated at a young age, they tend to aspire to be a part of the system when grown up. Making teenagers and young adults attend dinner table business discussions and taking their help in small business activities are the ways some families have trained them. Sharing family's stories, incidents and photographs and making them visit the office/workplace occasionally builds familiarity with the business environment.

Succession planning for gen-next is not about filling the board position and transferring ownership rights. It is about transferring family values and legacy, leading the organization and taking it to the next level. Raising their ambition and motivation is a sure way to catch them young.

Build Capabilities

In the 21st century, companies have to be extremely competitive in order to survive and thrive in global markets. Successors have to demonstrate their business acumen, adaptability and entrepreneurial spirit to perform and prosper.

A leader, not just by birth but by meritocracy, is respected by his people and the business community. For gen-next successors, it is necessary to develop managerial and leadership skills along with emotional intelligence. A well-planned on-boarding and orientation programme help them to build their competencies and capabilities. Nowadays, mentors and coaches are specialized in developing capabilities of gen-next scions.

Align Family and Business Interests

Succession planning is complicated when the family does not have a shared vision and the interests of members are not aligned.

Each family business has its unique culture and set of beliefs. When family members have incongruent aspirations and goals, it is challenging to develop common goals and specific roles. The key to avoiding such situations is to create a culture of good governance. Define what is the role of the family in business, what is the support the family can expect from the business, and what will be the policies and guidelines for family members for their contribution, expectations, performance, rewards, duties and inheritance.

In the VUCA world, it is the innovative and professional work culture that will entice gen-next to be in the business to continue the legacy.

WILL MANY GENERATIONS IN FAMILY BUSINESS BECOME A DREAM?

The American entomologist and biologist Edward O. Wilson (2012) said: 'We have created a Star Wars civilisation, with Stone Age emotions, medieval institutions and Godlike technology'. This is the sort of combination we are seeing today, and that is why we need innovation and need to have inclusiveness as we look ahead. It is a highly turbulent and disruptive world!

There are companies in Europe and Japan which have lasted for 16 generations and more. Not many companies, but a large number are going on to four to six generations. And we are all filled with admiration for such companies. We are also witnessing a spurt in gen-next led enterprises. The second generation of Jains—twins Anuraag and Tarang—have built two companies (Endurance and Varroc), both in non-competing auto components, into billion dollar corporations. Initially, they leveraged their uncle Rahul Bajaj's lineage, where Bajaj group is India's powerhouse of the auto/scooter industry. Then they flowered into corporations not entirely dependent on their family connection—and now employing thousands of people across India and Europe. They seem to be seamlessly moving towards the third generation.

Another case is of Goenkas, the founding family of Tally Solutions. They revamped sales and support network of India's oldest software product outfit. It matters a great deal in the GST era. Tejas Goenka started the company in 1986 and is moving forward now with the help of his 28-year-old son, who is both competent and enthusiastic about growing the business. Tally has 1.5 million licensed customers, and it is estimated that there are 5 million who pirate the software.

Musings

In February 2018, Cox and Kings celebrated their 260th anniversary in Delhi, India. This travel agency has transformed from a British-owned to a second-generation Indian-owned organization and is said to be the oldest travel agency in the world. Cox and Kings claim to be the leaders in innovation in travel and has several firsts to its name: chartering a special plane to view the longest solar eclipse in the 21st century; introducing Russia's first luxury train—the Bolshoi Express—launching state-of-the-art luxury railway journeys in India, offering special packages to the world's largest pilgrimage—the Maha Kumbh Mela—and some more, all under Peter Kerkar, following in the footsteps of his father Ajit Kerkar.

GEN-NEXT CARVING THEIR OWN PATH

In this VUCA world, there will be less and less talk about generations carrying the flag, the same flag as earlier generations did. There will be more like Azim Premji and Harsh Mariwala who changed the direction of the business or the business itself on inheriting from their parents. There will be more like Bill Gates who are starters and then hand over the business to professionals to take the company forward.

With the millennial generation, heirs of some of the India's tycoons have charted their own entrepreneurial path instead of joining their family businesses. Ananya Birla has become a social entrepreneur and runs Svatantra Microfinance venture successfully. Parth Jindal could have taken the reins of the multi billion dollar empire—JSW group. He chose to start JSW ventures, a technology venture capital fund of ₹1 billion, with an objective of diversification. Rishabh Mariwala, son of Harsh Mariwala, chose to carve out his own path by joining Soap Opera N More, a venture that sells niche hand-made soaps, a brainchild of his mother Archana Mariwala.

There will always be the odd exception. They are the phoenix companies that rise again after one or even many falls, like the Agnelli family that runs the Fiat empire. Founded in 1899, at one time, the Agnelli empire was 5% of the GDP of Italy. And then the wars, lack of capital and increased competition from rest of Europe happened. The determination of the Agnelli family not to let the banks take over and their commitment was shown by them putting all their accumulated wealth into saving the company And their ability to let some of them take on responsibility for management, and the others remaining behind and giving support, Fiat now has a much large stable of products, own and acquired to stay afloat in the VUCA environment.

We may see more and more companies' life cycles reducing to perhaps one generation—the founder only. It is not because the company was not successful. It could even be that the company was very successful. And then the founder moves on. And the company moves on. Each adjusting to the changing world defined by VUCA.

Do not go where the path may lead, go instead where there is no path, and leave a trail.

Ralph Waldo Emerson

GOVERNANCE
Enhancing Value

❝ *If management is about
running the business,
governance is about seeing
that it is run properly.*

Robert Ian Tricker **❞**

GOVERNANCE: THE FOURTH G OF 5G SUCCESS FRAMEWORK

The world's largest corporate scam, Enron, happened in 2001. One of the biggest energy traders and supplier companies in the USA became extremely successful in a short time and then spiralled down to bankruptcy. The massive accounting fraud wiped out $78 billion in stock market value and led to the collapse of Arthur Andersen, one of the top five global accounting firms.

From the time of Mahabharata (3000 BCE), we have read and heard stories of manipulation, cheating, frauds and bribery in the family, business and anything in between. Today in the VUCA world, cases of corporate scams and unethical business dealings do not surprise us. Enron is merely one example of the 21st century's wrong practices of promoters, hand-in-hand with the auditors—the financial record keepers and checkers. There are many more and will be, till human beings are driven by greed and fear.

Unscrupulous practices of a few impact many in terms of huge financial losses to investors, livelihood of employees and dents in the world economy. Integrity and ethics are the values we praise and preach about. Yet in the world of business—of corporates and of family enterprises—we find countless examples of sheer abuse of these values.

Governance, the fourth G, is a critical element for the longevity and success of family businesses. It ensures that family values and business goals are synchronized. When governance is the *code of conduct* for shareholder families, not only do the

THE 5Gs OF FAMILY BUSINESS

customers and employees get benefited but also the other stakeholders and society at large. Such family businesses build their legacies for generations.

GOVERNANCE IN VUCA WORLD

In his book *Centuries of Success*, William O' Hara wrote: 'Before the multinational corporation, there was family business. Before the Industrial Revolution, there was family business. Before the enlightenment of Greece and the empire of Rome, there was family business' (Cruz 2016).

For omnipresent family businesses, ownership and continuity are the key features. Conventionally, an individual founder or the family owns and controls the business. In the VUCA world, the concept of family's ownership has expanded to modern corporates with shared ownership. These are legal entities with owner-promoters' shareholding (equity) as the capital. Investors can invest by trading in the company's shares publicly. Companies can issue new shares to raise capital for future investment. Stock exchanges are the trading platforms for such transactions.

For such publicly traded companies, managing the business in a fair and transparent manner is obligatory. A professional board of directors is responsible for seeing the operations and ensuring good governance practices. In some cases, owner-ship and management control are separated as per regulatory guidelines but the control is still retained with promoters. Some of these companies become fertile ground for corruption, scams and frauds.

In UK, there were 'scandalous' collapse of several prominent companies during the late 1980s and the early 1990s. A committee was set up following the raft of governance failures.

Chaired by Sir Adrian Cadbury, the Financial Aspects of Corporate Governance Committee, proposed governance measures. The Cadbury committee defined corporate governance as 'the system by which companies are directed and controlled'. More specifically, it is the tested operating framework for managing relationships among members of the management team; the board of directors; controlling shareholders; minority shareholders; and also other stakeholders of the company.[1]

In the USA, the genesis of the Enron scam led to the Sarbanes-Oxley Act in 2002. It came into existence to enhance governance and bring transparency in financial and managerial dealings to combat fraud, improve reliability of financial reporting and restore investor confidence in corporates. The Act specifies that it is the management's responsibility to maintain a sound internal-control structure for financial reporting and to assess its own effectiveness, and it is the auditors' responsibility to 'take control of controls' by attesting the soundness of the management's assessment and reporting on the overall financial control system (Wagner and Dittmar 2006).

In India, the first corporate governance code for companies—'Desirable Corporate Governance: A Code'—was drafted under the chairmanship of Rahul Bajaj. In 2000, SEBI constituted the Kumar Mangalam Birla Committee to draft a code of corporate governance. In 2017, the Uday Kotak Committee released a report on corporate governance. Each report has been an attempt to enhance quality of corporate governance, and thereby increase the value of shareholders' investment.

When families or promoters aspire to separate management control from ownership, governance becomes a crucial aspect,

---

[1]See https://www.applied-corporate-governance.com/definition-of-corporate-governance/, accessed 25 June 2018.

leading to formalizing structures, processes, decision flow and power—for business and for family. In the era of mergers, acquisitions and private equity funding, there are some businesses where the promoter or family's voting control is much diluted, though the family name, reputation and culture still prevail. Some of the Tata and Mahindra group companies are highly profitable and reputed, though the promoters' stakes are miniscule.

Musings

One evening a Chinese traveller came to meet Chanakya (Kautilya). It was dusk, and Chanakya was writing some important papers under the light of an oil lamp. Electricity was not invented then. Chanakya welcomed his visitor and asked him to sit.

Chanakya quickly finished his work. Then he extinguished the oil lamp under which he was working and lit another lamp. The visitor was surprised. He asked Chanakya, whether it was a custom in India to extinguish a lamp and light another when a guest arrives at home.

Chanakya replied, 'No my friend. There is no such custom. When you entered I was doing an official work pertaining to my country. The oil filled in that lamp has been bought from the money from the National treasury. Now our conversation is personal, not related to my country. So I cannot use that lamp now, as it will be a wastage of money of the National treasury. So I extinguished the lamp and lit the another, since oil in this lamp has been bought from my personal money'.

We live in a global capitalist society. Will we succeed in the VUCA world with governance and ethics, an ingrained part of our social and business culture?

NUANCES OF GOVERNANCE IN FAMILY BUSINESS

Governance is the key to build and sustain a robust and respectable ownership model for families. It is the action or the manner to control, direct or strongly impact the conduct of the organization. Family business founders—patriarchs—do not consider themselves as 'governing' the business and the family. For them, governance mirrors their values reflected in the culture of family business.

Governance applies to every area of the operation, encompassing family as an organization, business as an organization and the interaction between the two. The simplest way to describe it may be in the statement, *that is not the way we do it over here.*

Empirical research and global studies show that family-controlled businesses are better managed, and they outperform non-family businesses in several ways. There is more emphasis on quality and value-for-money for customers because it is a matter of family's reputation and name. Leadership is long tenured, unlike the movement of CEOs with an average tenure of 5–7 years. Focus is not just on quarterly performance, but on sustainable strategies.

Entrepreneurship and innovation are a part of the culture of family businesses. They treat employees with fairness and loyalty, and expect the same in return. There is a strong sense of responsibility to society. Giving back—the contribution is not only of money but also of time and involvement by family members. Family businesses invest in the development of management skills for family as well as non-family employees.

On the other side, family businesses suffer from a shorter life span, with hardly 3% to 4% businesses surviving in the fourth generation. In spite of being India's wealth creators and assets builders, they are fragile and emotional. They get affected by family dynamics and conflict, largely because of lack of governance and lack of succession planning. Inadequate governance is the result of poor management control, weak systems and processes and unclear objectives and goals.

FAMILY BUSINESS COMPLEXITY

The uniqueness of family business is in its interaction and in its overlap of family and business—two systems. Renowned researchers Tagiuri and Davis (1996) developed a three-circle model of family business. They added 'ownership' as the third dimension. As shown in Figure 4.1, three independent yet overlapping systems—family, business and ownership—create seven distinct sectors. Any individual in a family business can be placed in one of the seven sectors.

FIGURE 4.1 THREE-CIRCLE MODEL OF THE FAMILY BUSINESS SYSTEM

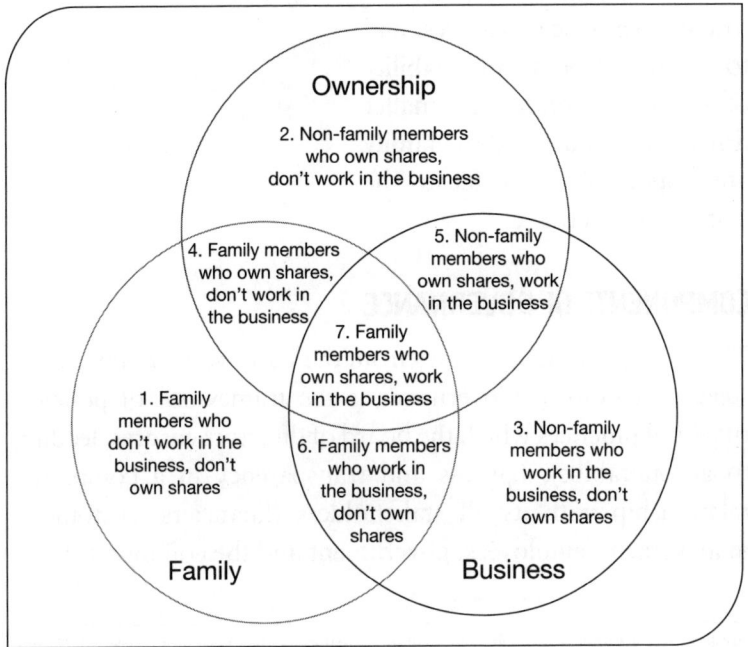

Source: Tagiuri and Davis (1996)

For example, in the family, some members work in the business and others don't. Some members own shares and others don't. Some members work as well as own shares. There may be non-family members who work in the business but do not own shares, or they work in the business and also own shares, or they do not work in the business but own shares.

When we look at the conceptual architecture of a family controlled business, such an overlap is tricky, complex and bound to create friction among entities of the seven sectors. To maintain harmony and equilibrium, clear guidelines and policies, roles, and accountability in the organization and within the family are obligatory.

A well-designed governance mechanism ensures that individuals in these seven sectors interact and support each other to keep family business effective and productive. In corporates, the board of directors is responsible for implementation and monitoring governance measures, and to ensure prosperity and viability of the organization. In smaller firms, the founder and the family are responsible to inculcate the culture of governance.

> 'Shelving hard decisions is the least ethical course'.
>
> **Adrian Cadbury**

COMPONENTS OF GOVERNANCE

The word governance comes from the Latin verb *gubernare*, to steer, or to direct. Governance is the framework of policies, rules and practices which the board of directors ensures, leading to accountability, fairness and transparency in a company's relationship with its all stakeholders (financiers, customers, management, employees, government and the community).[2]

---

[2]See http://www.businessdictionary.com/definition/corporate-governance.html, accessed 25 June 2018.

The aim of governance is to define and develop a course of operations, a path for the good of the organization, the stakeholders and the promoters. In family businesses, governance has two overlapping components—corporate and family (Koeberle-Schmid, Kenyon-Rouvinez and Poza 2014).

Corporate Governance

Corporate governance is a concept that has been in existence since a long time. Chanakya's *Arthashastra*, an ancient Indian political treatise on statecraft, economic policy and military strategy, is considered the oldest document on governance. In a broad context, it is about maintaining the overall framework of governance, rather than on specific interventions in people's lives. The treatise repeatedly states that self-restraint is the single-most important attribute in a king. In other words, the Kautilyan ideal is a 'strong' but 'limited' state.[3]

Today, for ambitious business families, the strategic roadmap is to go on a public listing route. It gives finance required for growth and diversification, and also helps in reducing the overall cost of capital and interest costs on existing debt. We may say, almost since the first company listed on the first public market, capitalist business owners have pursued to raise money without sacrificing control.

Adrian Cadbury said,

> [C]orporate governance is concerned with holding the balance between economic and social goals and between individual and communal goals. The governance framework is there to encourage efficient use of resources and

---

[3]See https://blogs.economictimes.indiatimes.com/et-commentary/why-india-needs-to-no-longer-be-an-ashokan-republic-but-a-chanakyan-one/, accessed 25 June 2018.

equally to require accountability for the stewardship of those resources. The aim is to align as nearly as possible the interests of individuals, corporations and society.

Professional management of the business takes place through the board of directors, elected by the shareholders or appointed by other board members. They represent the shareholders. Many a time, majority shareholding is with promoters and their family members, and therefore the board has most positions represented by family members.

The dichotomy is that when promoters and their families have a strong foundation of values and ethics, they consider themselves as the trustees of the business. Over a period, family businesses become institutions of stature. On the other hand, weaker values and compromised ethics lead to scams, corruption and loss of enterprise value.

Musings

Founders and their families often exert extraordinary power over public companies, even when they own only a minority of the shares. They may still be the largest single shareholder, unless smaller shareholder groups 'coalesce' to create 'a majority block'. According to the corporate laws in every country, the shareholding rights and voting controls differ. One such example is of the Porsche and Piëch families having total voting control over the German car company Volkswagen, despite owning only half of its equity. The publicly traded shares, providing the other half of Porsche's capital, have no right to vote.

Family Governance

With the business life cycle, the family's life cycle also changes. The family's orientation towards business, either family-first or business-first, plays an important role in the long-term strategies and continuity. It is necessary that the families follow a few principles such as fairness, inclusiveness and responsible ownership for healthy sustenance.

Family governance is about managing the family, and following policies and norms so that the family's values are preserved, principles are followed and harmony is maintained, especially when the family transition happens from siblings state to cousins consortium.

As Suresh Kotak, the 84-year-old 'cotton man of India' and one of the oldest family in cotton trading, says, 'the family business is a good place to learn, but it can get very rigorous. Ours was definitely not a papa ka business'. His son Uday has charted out a new career path in finance industry and is a prominent Indian banker who has headed the Uday Kotak Committee on Corporate Governance.

Family governance can be implemented as a tool, as a mechanism with a structure, processes, policies, norms and guidelines. The purpose is to facilitate interaction among family members, and provide a platform for constructive discussion and problem-solving. The family's relationship with the business needs to be defined. It increases transparency and accountability by inculcating professional attitude and approach in owner-promoters, the board of directors and other decision-makers. Family governance is the way of living rather than just adhering to documents and policies.

PERILS OF NON-GOVERNANCE

In a family-owned business, the centre of control is more powerful than in the non-family corporate. It allows for concessions and gives a long leash for possible wrongdoings. Add to that a business environment of mild to severe exploitation and corruption at different levels. The leaders could have a heady cocktail of power and ego which may sometimes be difficult to resist. This is in spite of written policies and manuals which clearly specify what can and cannot be done, in spite of internal audit and external audit, in spite of independent directors on the board, and in spite of well-defined systems, checks and balances that companies introduce.

The Independent directors who are expected to be the whistle blowers are at times found to be the friends of owner-promoters, under their influence or obligations, and well paid. Often women family members—close or distant relatives—are appointed to the board only due to regulatory requirements. They are neither trained nor expected to contribute in the boardroom discussions. The temptation for internal trading is too strong to resist, and a small group which includes the top management can manage it without even a whiff of suspicion. The more successful the company, the higher the unjustified rewards.

Such situations have been with owner-promoters such as Ramalinga Raju of Satyam Computers, Vijay Mallya of United Spirits, Nirav Modi the Diamondtaire and others, who have managed to suck the company and leave the shareholders facing a blank wall. Such scams happen and will keep repeating, not only in India but globally as well.

Thomas Jefferson has stated, 'in estimating every man's value either in private or public life, a pure integrity is the quality we take first into calculation, and that learning and talents are only the second'.

CULTURE OF GOVERNANCE

What can be done to prevent gaps in governance and scams in the future from family businesses?

There is a need to develop a culture that is deeply rooted in the values of discipline, transparency and objectivity. There is a need to establish well-designed systems and processes, a robust mechanism of checks and balances to identify gaps in the system and take corrective steps.

It is difficult to define 'culture' in an organization, but it is easy to describe 'culture' from what is seen and felt—evident from the way employees in the organization behave. Culture is often determined by the leader, the entrepreneur-patriarch of the family. It carries an imprint for many years, perhaps even for many generations. It does not happen in the non-family corporates where the imprint of the CEO does get stamped, but it is temporary and transient. In some situations where the CEO has been there for a long time, as with Jack Welch in GE, or Alfred Sloan of GM, or A. Naik of L&T, the stamp is greater, more marked and lasting, than during the standard tenure of most corporate CEOs.

Culture defines *how things are done here and how they are expected to be done*. Governance clarifies *what is not done here*. Culture is a derivative of the beliefs and values that are interwoven with one's personality, and which becomes so apparent that the onlooker can create an identity. It happens with nations, with corporates, family businesses and business leaders.

We need examples where the younger generation observes that their seniors did not go for the low-hanging fruit even though easily available, because it was wrong. We need leaders who lay high emphasis on integrity. Such examples are seldom forgotten.

When J.R.D. Tata was chairman of Air India (AI) and had to go to London urgently at short notice, he found that the AI flight was full with only one economy seat available. He took it. He refused all adjustments that the crew wanted to make, insisted on the food for economy class passengers and alighted in London the following day, having taught a lesson to the crew by example rather than a sermon!

When Azim Premji refused to pay 'facilitating payment' for clearance of some urgently required computer parts and agreed to pay higher demurrage payment, he was believed to have taken a less attractive decision. All Wipro staff heard about this incident and knew that they were expected to do likewise, in case such situations arose.

Values, built into a culture through examples and company lore, and which make family and employees proud, that they only do it this way, is what good governance is all about, an essential element in the 5Gs for family business.

Take the case of a nation, Japan, where a culture of high integrity is so evident. Japan is known for its minor earthquakes. A few years ago in Tokyo, sudden tremors were felt during the day. Shoppers ran out of shops and malls, and headed home for safety. The next morning, there were long queues at the shopping centres. The shoppers had come to declare what they had taken the previous evening and to pay for these purchases. They were waiting in queues in the hot sun! *Culture*.

When Parry, the old revered British company, known as a 'boxwalla company' was taken over by the Murugappa group, there was a culture shock. The new chairman was always in white shirt sleeves. The managers who always wore a suit and tie to work now looked odd in the corporate office. The long lunch break in the executive lunch room became shorter and simpler without waiter's services. There was no time now for even a short siesta. It was just a 'lunch break' now, not a long 'break'. Leaving a little early in the evening to play a round of golf was out of the question. Parry had changed. It was a new, simple and entirely work-oriented culture. It was seen as a crying need in the context of the poor financial results of Parry over the past few years! *Culture*.

There is the 'high integrity' culture of the Tata group, greatly reinforced during the long tenure of J.R.D. Tata—the chairman who always set a 'humane and human' example. Discouraging the payment of bribes to facilitate business, waiting with his guests for his turn to get a table at the restaurant owned by the Tata group, making sure that the driver was not delayed beyond work time, and allowing the driver's children (and their friends) to play in the garden at his home— J.R.D. set a standard of nobility with humility! *Culture*.

When the leader of the family business projects a culture across the whole organization, generally, the culture gets deeply rooted with succeeding generations. Therefore, changing it to tune-up with current times has to be done smartly and slowly. Then there is no upheaval and shock and response of 'this is not how it is done here'. Why? *Culture*.

CUSTOMS: THE FOUNDATION OF GOVERNANCE

There is the internationally operating Kewalram Chanrai group, about 150 years old. They are the originators of well-known brands like Reddington and Olam, one of the world's largest companies in the field of commodity trading. They have set up one of the top class hospitals—Jaslok Hospital in Mumbai.

The promoters from the fifth generation play an advisory role and oversee finance but leave business operations spanning 12 countries to professionals. Family governance is practised beyond any processes and formalities. When the mother Chanrai was alive, she lived in Mumbai. Her three sons, lived in different parts of the world. To give company to old mother, each brother used to visit Mumbai and stay with mother for three months at a stretch. They would get involved in the hospital trust's activities as philanthropy was a core value of the family. Love and respect for the mother were in sync with business objectives. It was a family in business.

The Harilela Group is amongst the wealthiest families in Hong Kong. The family of Indian origin has settled in Hong Kong since the 1930s and is into diverse businesses, including the Holiday Inn. The Harilela brothers live in the vicinity with the patriarch Hari Harilela's house being the main family house. Harilelas follow an unwritten rule that every Sunday, all the family members would have lunch at the main house, unless they are out of town. Guests visiting the brothers and cousins are also invited for lunch.

This ritual gives an opportunity to all the members of the family, now many through four generations, to meet and discuss and keep in touch. The Harilelas have an unseen bond binding them and keeping them close as a family. An example of family governance in practice!

PROFESSIONALIZATION: THE BACKBONE OF GOVERNANCE

For most family business leaders-patriarchs, to balance three systems—family-business-ownership—is crucial. The analysis of how do these systems overlap will provide pointers to the kind of balances the family has to work out to manage a successful operation and without much conflict.

Asian Paints, one of India's most successful companies has left imprints in many parts of the world without blowing horns and drawing attention to themselves. They have worked out transitions. A public listed company with a majority share-holding of the founding Choksi, Dani and Vakil families, the management is totally professional with a non-family managing director and CEO at the helm. Likewise, the Burman family of Dabur India, in its fifth generation, has professionalized the management. Family members would remain on the board only as investors. There are many glaring examples of corporate India where families have worked out an ideal balance between objectivity from professional work culture and a certain closeness that comes with family ownership.

In a VUCA environment, the leaders have to be VUCA prepared. Family businesses face a daunting challenge of attracting and retaining professionals to give an impetus to business.

In a quest of hiring qualified and experienced, and cost-effective human resources, business owners tend to overlook personal aspirations and values of employees.

As Warren Buffett says,

> [Y]ou're looking for three things, generally, in a person—intelligence, energy, and integrity. And if they don't have the last one, don't even bother with the first two. Everyone here has the intelligence and energy—you wouldn't be here otherwise. But the integrity is up to you. You weren't born with it, you can't learn it in school (Schwantes 2018).

Hiring the right people, and creating a conducive environment for them to work and lead can help owner families save money, and grow the business smoothly and efficiently.

Musings

170 years ago, Werner von Siemens[4] started the business of dynamo machines and electrical engineering. Over a period, several of his brothers began working for the company. The close relationship among three Siemens brothers—Werner, William and Carl, working respectively in Berlin, London and St. Petersburg—gave rise to a multinational family-run company that well understood what to do with the opportunities offered by the age's first wave of globalization.

The original partnership had only 10 employees in 1887, and went on to become a multinational giant, the world's one of the top electrical company. Siemens was able to do all this because he focused not on short-term gain, but on creating something that would last with a strong sense of belongingness. The ultimate currency that counted for him was 'receiving recognition of the rightness of my actions and the usefulness of my work'.

---

[4]See https://www.siemens.com/history/en/news/1051_werner_von_siemens.htm

Good governance can be ensured in many ways, but it is the spirit behind it that is important. The corollary is when the torch of family pride is held high, it ensures governance and best practices.

WHAT IS FAIR AND FOR WHOM

Long-term continuity of a family business depends on the emotional involvement and engagement of family members. However, VUCA forces are bound to create an unstable and ambiguous environment, a fertile ground for conflict—in business and in family.

Many a time, decisions in the family are taken by the patriarch with or without the consent of other members. Aspirations and desires of some family members are compromised in favour of other members. Sacrifices are expected and egos are clashed. Family as a system is softer and sentimental compared to the rational business system.

Interpersonal dynamics, communication gaps and a sense of entitlement by younger generation can lead to inequality and injustice among family members. For success and progress, it is vital that the family defines fair processes in dealing with each other.

When founders have built business empires consisting many companies, in many industries, the dilemma of succession is obvious. How to plan for succession, whom to prepare to take the leadership baton, especially when there are more than one successors? Companies are not like apples which can be sliced into equal parts and then distributed, again in equal parts, to the three or four or even two children involved. The companies have complex structures and different turnovers, profits and future growth projections, and therefore different valuations. Children, the potential successors, also have different aptitudes and attitudes, different IQs and EQs, and different capabilities and capacities, which have to be fitted into the business of the company they may inherit to avoid square pegs in round holes. Here is where founder-entrepreneurs, at the end of their working lives, come to the 'decision-making crossroads'.

One of India's oldest and top business houses of Birla was built by the great entrepreneur G.D. Birla for over 40 years. It was carved into four sections by him as his succession plan, with full disclosure. It was not exactly an equal share, because he took into account the capability of each of his three sons. In fact, he broke his own rule and gave the fourth share to his favourite grandson Aditya, in whom he saw a reflection of himself. Thirty years since then, all the sections are either coasting along or drowning, except the one headed by his grandson. Aditya Birla's section has grown by leaps and bounds. In some industries such as aluminium, carbon black, polyester fibre, they are among the leaders in the world.

One may say that the allocation, which was 'close to fair' to the sons, was not fair to the employees or the shareholders or the community as most of the companies did not do well. The owners (and indeed the founder) did owe an obligation to these three groups as well! And this does not include 'customers'—a group that cannot be ignored, especially when Peter Drucker kept repeating 'the only purpose for the existence of a company is to create and keep a customer'. In all the concentration and confusion of sharing the wealth of the corporation, the primary segment of customers which helped to create the wealth is somehow ignored.

Many corporations have disappeared by the third generation, with such fragmentation done to satisfy 'fair distribution objectives'. Therefore, it would seem that the distribution of shareholding in the form of ESOPs (employee stock owner-ship plan) or other similar ways could work better rather than paying only fixed remuneration for operational control to professionals. Rewarding those who occupy positions based on 'meritocracy', rather than on 'genealogy', may seem to be the best solution! As Steve Job said, 'it doesn't make sense to hire smart people and then tell them what to do; we hire smart people so they can tell us what to do'.

There may be the entrepreneurial gene transmitted, like in the case of Aditya Birla, where he created a castle from the small mansion that he had inherited. Or there may be an L.N. Mittal, who took his share and parted from his steelmaker father and family, and went on his own to start operations in Indonesia and graduated to become the steel king of the world!

There are exceptions—and may their tribe increase! For the rest, they have to look at other solutions which are fair to all stakeholders, who have helped to bring the corporation to the level of success that it has achieved.

ABSOLUTE POWER CORRUPTS ABSOLUTELY

The quote 'absolute power corrupts absolutely' is from British politician Lord Acton, which has been repeated so often that it has become synonymous with the subject of power.

Entrepreneurs, especially in the first generation when they have total or majority ownership of the enterprise that they have founded, also have absolute power. Whether they use it with restraint, for their good and the good of the community, or whether they misuse this power, is what distinguishes the 'good' from the 'evil'.

An example of the latter is Ramalinga Raju, who was an early IT czar of India, and who was convicted on 9 April 2015 to 7 years in jail and a fine of $1 million for an accounting fraud of $100 billion. It caused a notional loss to investors of $200 billion, and gave an unlawful gain to Raju and his partners in a crime of $30 billion. They were all convicted of criminal conspiracy, criminal breach of trust, cheating, using false documents and falsification of accounts.

Raju had founded Satyam Computers in 1987 with 20 employees. When the scandal broke out in 2008, Satyam had 40,000 employees, 185 Fortune 500 clients and operations in 66 countries. He had won many accolades including the E&Y Award for Entrepreneur of the Year. Just months before his confession in 2009, Satyam bagged the prestigious international corporate governance award!

Entrepreneurial success had changed Raju. He had insatiable greed to own land. It is said that he had real estate properties in 63 countries. He syphoned off money from Satyam to buy more and more land, and when land values slumped, he was in a severe problem. He also got tempted to live a lavish lifestyle—with 321 pairs of shoes, 310 belts, and 13 cars including Mercedes and BMW. He had a priceless telescope installed at his home.

Had Satyam been wholly owned by Raju, there would have been less of a problem. But Satyam had got listed in 1992, and was oversubscribed 17 times! A subsidiary, Satyam Infoway, was listed on NASDAQ and traded at the double its face value on the first day. Satyam also followed with an ADR issue. After seeing this substantial flow of cash, Raju started fudging the books from 2001 and artificially increasing the share price. In 2006, Raju claimed Satyam had crossed the

$1 billion mark in revenues. In the meantime, he reduced the promoters share in Satyam from 80% in 2001 to nearly 0% in 2008. He made sure that only the unsuspecting investors lost!

Another well-known case is of Bernard Madoff, an American stockbroker and a fraudster. It is a sad story of how a successful entrepreneur climbed to great heights and ended up in prison because of his gross indiscretion and greed.

The blessing in disguise in this scam was that the government asked the Institute of Chartered Accountants and the Institute of Company Secretaries to probe the role of auditors and company secretaries. The focus also shifted to the role of audit firms and independent directors for whistleblowing. The new Companies Act 2013 provided for stricter corporate governance provisions and responsible board management to ensure such scams do not occur again.

BUILDING PROCESSES TO MANAGE CONFLICT

Research on conflict in family business suggests that certain causes of conflict are quite detrimental, and could damage relationships and businesses. Lack of a unified vision and common objectives and entry of gen-next in the business, especially if not planned, are two major causes of conflict in a family business. At times, influence of outsiders on some family members and inability of the leader to be perceived as trustworthy, and fair, can also lead to breakups and splits.

How to mitigate conflict? There are three steps to build processes that can manage triggers of conflict, especially in case of families with business orientation

First, the family has to develop a family constitution with explicable rules and policies of ownership, succession and distribution of shareholding, and rules for exit. *Second,* there has to be a structured body like the board of directors or Council of Advisors to ensure the compliance of rules and policies. *Third,* transparency and 'buy in' of all family members to accept decisions and follow the Code of Conduct as defined collectively.

Godrej, Murugappa, GMR group, Burmans of Dabur and several other prominent business families have developed fair processes and implemented their family constitution, guiding their fourth and fifth generations to stay on course.

MANAGING SUCCESSION

'Each succeeding generation sees the family business not as a matter of ownership, but of trusteeship', says A. Vellayan, the current executive chairman of Murugappa Group (Sagar and Vasudeva 2017). The fifth generation has joined the business, and still the family is 'all together'.

Murugappa Group has achieved this distinction. How have they done it?

A noteworthy example is M.V. Subbiah. Four years into his tenure as the chairman of Murugappa Group, M.V. Subbiah was, in a way, *demoted*. He was requested by the board to step down and make way for his cousin M.A. Alagappan as the new chairman. It was a decision of the board which included three independent directors. Subbiah says, 'I was if you prefer, demoted. But in the interest of the family and the way you are brought up with family values, you step down and allow that to happen'. He also added, 'I could have continued as chairman if I wanted to, but then, I might have broken the family'. Here is a stunning example of practising values for harmony in family and growth of business.

The life expectancy of the family business is quite low as per statistics. It is often said that 'the first generation grows it; the second generation enjoys it; the third generation destroys it'. Barely 3% of businesses reach the fourth generation.

Apparently, with a combination of a shared vision, pride in the family name, pursuing agreed goals, allowing each person to match his talents and inclinations to what is required in the business, differences can be managed within the family. Harmony prevails with respect for one another in-spite of age difference, and with an inborn culture where money is not the driving force in the family.

The individuals have not gone 'soft' over the generations with pelf and power—which happens to most families. Great credit must be given to the generations old families who have carried the torch, proudly!

Most families begin their breakups right in the second generation. Cadila Laboratories in Ahmedabad was started by two friends, who had graduated from L.M. College of Pharmacy, I.A. Modi and Raman Patel. The company went from strength to strength and became one of the leading companies in the pharma industry.

A consultant who first visited Cadila factory had to break the meeting for lunch. Modi took him to the canteen, the only one where they had lunch with all the factory workers and the drivers and peons. The same food and same ambience for the owner as well as the gatekeeper! The consultant was impressed. It was in the 1980s, and such equalizers were rarely seen. In those days, the class distinction between owners, managers and workers existed. Eating facilities and toilets were separate for directors, managers and general staff, in Indian companies, even at the multinationals and large agency houses.

However, when Modi and Patel died, the children did not get along as well as their parents did. So they separated and each started their own company in the same business—Zydus Cadila and Cadila Care. Both have professionalized their companies and are doing exceptionally well. Zydus has also expanded into high-quality hospital care.

There are others like the Piramal family where two brothers, Ajay and Dilip, parted the company. Ajay Piramal moved into real estate, pharma and venture capital, and Dilip moved into baggage. Both have done well, with Ajay having grown rapidly into being one of the leading industrialists in India.

There are family companies that pre-empt problems by separating shareholding from operational responsibilities in time before any damage is done. However, this requires the patriarch to be a sensitive visionary and an excellent judge of capabilities.

Musings

Merck group was founded in 1668 and is the world's oldest operating chemical and pharmaceutical company, as well as one of the largest pharmaceutical companies in the world, now into the 14th generation. The family has charted out a powerful governance mechanism and has separated ownership from management control. The family of over 200 members has a structured family council and family board. Their involvement in the business is only to the extent of providing overall guidance and upholding the founder's values in firms across the world.

IN-LAWS AND OUTLAWS

In-laws have a special social relationship with the family. Social customs specify that in-laws have to be treated with decorum, formality and respect. Much less in the 21st century, though about 50 and more years ago, the trend of not accepting casual hospitality or favours from in-laws was common. For instance, a father may not even drink a glass of water at his daughter's family house (Dutta 1997). Norms of obligations and responsibilities were different for in-laws of sons and daughters. Such social connotations and conventions had evolved from the joint family system where prestige, social strata and caste-community belongingness were crucial for business. Such customs, perhaps broadly defined the governance mechanism in the family and society.

With influence of global social culture and Western lifestyle, the implication of the 'in-laws' relationship has radically changed. Now in-laws are considered a part of the extended family; yet most business families refrain from having in-laws in ownership of the business.

One exception to such a custom is Anand Rathi, a leading stock broking and financial advisory firm in Mumbai. They have a joint family structure of in-laws. Anand Rathi's son, daughter, son-in-law and his father, all are engaged in the business as promoters of several companies under the brand Anand Rathi. The in-laws in partnership!

When family's inheritance and wealth distribution has to take place, many families insist that such a matter is sensitive and has to be discussed in a closed room among siblings only. Spouses and in-laws are not a party to the discussion. As facilitators, external advisors are invited for the discussion.

In one of the families, the eldest member insisted this as a pre-condition. He was the leader of the business enterprise started by his father. His rationale was that the five siblings knew the family history, the ups and downs they had gone through, who among them can help, did help, or needed help from the others. There was a past that they shared. The life's journey that they went through together as siblings could not be fully disclosed or even would make no sense to spouses who had joined the family much later. Therefore, in all probability, they would always have a short-term and immediate family view on all decisions taken. The in-laws can never be an integral part of past family history.

Later, the leader acknowledged that it was the best decision taken. Discussions took place in context to the past and ended well. Perhaps not to the satisfaction of all as this is seldom possible. All the siblings were convinced that the allocations were fair, and there was no dirty linen exposed to the vulgar gaze of the lately come multitude.

THE TRUSTED ADVISOR

From the literature on family business advisory and our own experience, we find that there are at least two situations where intervention help and guidance from an external consultant, can be of great use.

One is the time of a start-up, a new venture. The founder is subsumed by his vision and his passion. In the process, the founder may miss out some important aspects of business strategies or actions.

Surveys have found that nearly 45% of start-ups fail because the product offering did not match the needs or wants of the customer. Another 40% fail because the start-up does not have all the skills needed to run the business successfully. The founder tries to 'do it all', and then flounders, and the project fails.

It is the reason for the advice from Narayan Murthy, the co-founder of Infosys, India's second largest IT company, as he says, 'the founder should always try and gather a group of people to help him, those who know what he does not know'. In fact, that is what Murthy did when he started Infosys. He selected a team that would provide expertise which is complementary to his strengths.

The second situation is where the owner-promoter is already a successor from second or higher generation. Money and power is already earned. It may make the owner feel he is invincible (to himself), and worse, can make him arrogant or risk-averse, losing out on growth opportunities. He may not be qualified and competent to play his role in changing phases, and may not have proven himself. So much worse as more help is needed from experts!

Such situations are rampant in family businesses, especially in the VUCA environment. In these circumstances, families can do with some outside help. Inputs from trusted advisors in the realm of family governance, conflict management, business strategies, wealth management, etc. can work well as they bring to the table not just management expertise, but more importantly, a balance of theory, concepts and practical experience. Management consultants have the ability to look at the problem dispassionately and find a solution. On the part of the family, inviting such intervention needs large dollops of humility, acceptance of 'I don't know' and objectivity of 'I know only what I know'.

MENTORING FOR SKILLS BUILDING

Learning and practising governance is not only a skill but is also an art. Families, and particularly owner-promoters, tend to get confined into their skillsets over a period and lose track of how the times have changed.

Every business leader needs support from time to time. Family members require a facilitator-mentor to help them communicate effectively and manage conflict. Business families are now open to ideas from outside and prefer to be transparent, even at the risk of being vulnerable. A growing number of professional advisors are using proactive skills to help families develop their future roadmap, succession plan and create a family business mechanism.

To become VUCA compliant, new skills have to be learned with an open mind. Peter Drucker was a coach of CEOs for some of the biggest corporations in the USA, such as to Alfred Sloan of General Motors. There are renowned academicians and advisors holding hands of leaders and mentoring them. There are consulting firms—national and international—advising business and families on various challenges. Great care must be taken to ensure that there is a good fit between the trusted advisor and the family, at levels of both mind and heart. If this fit is absent, or cannot be developed, then it can be a debacle instead of a solution (Aronoff and Ward 1994).

Most business owners agree to the fact that the success of their family businesses depend on the professionals they choose to advise them on multiple matters such as management, strategy, family dynamics, succession, law and wealth management. Professional consultants are building expertise in the family business domain as the ambiguity and complexity in the business environment have increased tremendously.

FAMILY CONSTITUTION: GOOD GOVERNANCE IN ACTION

While India is on its path to becoming the youngest nation by 2020, a paradigm shift is taking place in the family business domain. The traditionally managed companies are moving to 'professionally managed' companies. Significant reasons are that the millennial successors are well-educated, have global exposure and are digital aficionados. They prefer businesses to be operated with modern management techniques, to build teams and to create a culture of governance. Instead of getting stalled in family disputes, conflict and non-productive practices, millennials prefer to experiment, innovate and take risks.

Family constitution is a mechanism to develop good governance practices in business owning families. Broadly, the constitution components are:

Purpose: Family vision, mission and values

Structure: Family council, family board, committees and family office

Business: Vision, strategic planning and purpose of the board of directors

Procedures: Meetings, communication, budgets, venture funding, shareholders meetings and next-gen training

Policies and statements: Ownership eligibility, entry and exit norms, family compensation, dividends and reserves, conflict of interest and code of conduct

Family Welfare: Education, housing, medical, vehicles, vacation and retirement

Writing a constitution and implementing it with family's agreement and involvement is a daunting task, though a must for large, multi-generational families. Prudent families who have built their businesses as long-lasting institutions such as Godrej, Murugappa, Burmans (Dabur), GMR and Wockhardt have created a culture of good governance in the family. The families have built their family constitution, a document that addresses policies, practices and procedures. It is a way to connect and infuse the values of the family into how the business is operated.

FAMILY OFFICE: MANAGING WEALTH

Governance is a way of life, not just a mechanism to improve communication and transparency in family and business interactions. It is embedded in the culture of the family fabric. Established, successful and wealthy families constantly face the challenge of preserving, managing and enhancing their wealth. A family constitution provides a platform for open communication and collective decision-making on wealth-related issues. Yet a specialized area has emerged for wealthy families to manage their wealth—family office.

Many ultra-high net worth individual (UHNWI) families have set up their family offices to manage and augment their inherited wealth in a structured manner. Family office is a centre for several services to be provided to large, geographically spread, wealthy families. It is an investment, liquidity management and administrative/concierge centre (Leach 2007).

Each family has its unique need and outlook for investment. Family office enables members to invest as a group by increasing buying power and reducing portfolio management costs. The objective of family office is to have a centralized unit where coordination of various disciplines involved in family's asset management can be done. Instead of relying on one or a few financial institutions, the family can get an advantage of specialized financial services.

Family office is a separate operation from the business, though family members participate in it with professionals. It has structured operations, with defined roles. Family offices set up funds for philanthropy as well as for start-ups. Ajay Piramal, Burmans, Aniruddh Damani, Mohandas Pai, Dr Ranjan Pai, Narayan Murthi, Harsh Mariwala, Murugappa, Azim Premji and more have set up funds to invest in start-ups.

In India, the family office concept is at a nascent stage, and business families are learning and experimenting with the family office concept. It is also a way to foster family commitment and vision, and to perpetuate family legacy.

Promoters' Prerogatives

Habil Khorakiwala, Chairperson of Wockhardt Hospitals

A second-generation business tycoon shares his views on family governance (excerpts from the book *Odyssey of Courage*).

There is now a growing awareness among heads of family businesses that they should in fact have more structured methods and systems for the management and growth of their business, wealth and assets. A range of issues come up in a family business. First, there are interpersonal issues—the father–son relationship, sibling rivalry, the role of the in-laws, gender relations, and so on. Second, there are issues pertaining to compensation and role. Third, there are issues around individual ambitions, skills, roles and responsibilities. Fourth are the issues related to the relationship between the family and professional managers. Finally, there are issues pertaining to succession planning.

'I was fortunate in that there was no such bickering and breakups in our family.

Members of each generation found a way of doing their own thing, as it were. When I took charge of Wockhardt, I was pretty much on my own. My cousin Juzer was part of Wockhardt for some time and then went on to manage his own business. So the issue of generational transitions and the division of business was handled relatively smooth across generations.

With Wockhardt, we not only went public at home and abroad, but we also became a global company with varied business interests. I first had to find a way to get each of my children involved in the company. The company needed their talent, and I was keen that they should step in. Once I ensured that, both Nafisa (my wife) and I felt we should ensure the smooth functioning of the family, and planned transitions across various businesses and activities. Moreover, observing the mayhem in Indian family businesses in the 1990s and after, I also felt we should have a proper structure and codes of conduct to carry our business forward.

I found that more progressive business families were adopting charters and constitutions, and laying the rules of doing business for all family members. I decided that we should have a family charter, a formal system of interaction within the family, a transparent and rational methodology for the sharing and distribution of wealth and profit and so on.

In 2012, I approached Ernst & Young, India, and Berjis Desai at the law firm J. Sagar Associates (JSA). In a matter like this, the consultant must not only know the family, but must be able to appreciate the family's value system and philosophy. Without the empathy and understanding, no consultant can come up with sound advice.

I told them I had three principal objectives: [first], whatever we put in place must be regarded by all as a fair system; second, it should leave no space for any mis-interpretation, misunderstanding and conflict of interest; [and] finally it should stand at the test of time.

It took us two years to arrive at a constitution because the existing templates that I found were inadequate for the purpose and objectives that I had in mind. We had to devote considerable time to discussing a variety of issues in great detail first within the family and then with the consultants. Any family governance system must last beyond a generation and must ensure long-term survival, keeping in focus the massive changes taking place in technology, the emergence of new markets, new knowledge in managing the business and creation of shareholder value. It should provide the space and opportunity to future generations to fulfil their chosen path. Wockhardt is just an option. They must be able to pursue a different path for which they should have financial accessibility.

Finally, we adopted the idea of a family charter, a family council and a succession plan. I felt I had already succeeded in ensuring gender balance and also defining the individual roles of my three children. The charter and council were needed for growing forward, and also to institutionalize many of the good practices that we had already I would be the chairman of the council and my three children its members. Nafisa is not a part of the council, nor are the spouses of my children. I preferred it that way to make the point that the council would focus only on business matters, so only those directly involved in the business would be its members. By keeping Nafisa out, I made that distinction between family and family council. I also had a long-established rule that none of our family's in-laws, including the spouses of my children, would work for the company. This was meant to avoid any conflict of interest or cross-connections in managing the business and at the same time maintain cordial family relations'.

GOVERNANCE: A GREATER PRIORITY FOR 21ST CENTURY ENTREPRENEURS

We have known entrepreneurs in the last 100 years who set up businesses which are run by their children and their grand-children without too many problems. As a result, the brick and mortar—automobile, engineering, food and beverage and pharmaceutical companies—have moved forward.

Evidently, the owners were improving businesses all the time, and also becoming larger, sometimes becoming international players and household names across the globe. The management of some of these companies was transferred from owner-promoters to professional managers. It was done by choice, like in Unilever; or due to scale, like with Ford; or due to the kind of business, like Disney; or peer pressure from others on the board, as in Boehringer.

However, the kind of businesses that are being set up in the 21st century are significantly different from the business of the past. We are now in the age of artificial intelligence where robots will soon become our trusted assistants!

Entrepreneurs are younger, generally better qualified and achieve success much faster. Their attachment to the company is tenuous and is seen by the way they are willing to sell out, and then begin again with another project and perhaps another success. These are the 'serial entrepreneurs'.

There was a time when most of the GDP of Indian economy was from agriculture; then it moved to manufacturing. Now, much of the GDP comes from services, in particular IT and retail industries. Even in our emerging economy, the service sector contributes more than 50%!

Snapdeal, an online retail marketing company, was founded in 2010 by Kunal Bhatia, a Wharton alumnus, and Rohit Bahl, an IIT Delhi alumnus. Snapdeal moved on from being a daily deal site (like Groupon) to be an online marketplace for products (like Flipkart, started a few years earlier). In the era of mergers and acquisitions, it was 'snap-detailed', merged with Flipkart, a rival, at a vast sum.

Bahl and Bhatia have done a flip to start another Kart, and these two young men are billionaires in their early 30s.

Flipkart is a fairytale story of another e-tailer. Founded by Sachin Bansal and Binny Bansal (not related as a family) in 2007. The company initially focused on book sales before expanding into other product categories such as consumer electronics, fashion, and lifestyle products. In May 2018, Walmart acquired Flipkart for $16 billion, a valuation of over $20 billion, which made it the world's biggest e-commerce deal.

In 2014, WhatsApp was sold to Facebook, after just five years of existence, for $19 billion, by entrepreneur Jan Kuom, who was turned down for a job in Google and Facebook only five years ago!

In the age of information technology, when the world has changed faster than at any other time in the history, the emphasis is on innovation, rapid implementation, attachment to the idea, but detachment from the enterprise. Where does vision for future generations of the family come in? Many of these new age billionaires have not even started their families!

However, there is one area which cannot be ignored. The area of good and effective governance. In the past, governance evolved slowly as the company grew. Systems got established only after the company achieved a reasonable size, perhaps over several decades. No longer. These new age enterprises need to have governance systems in place soon after they have got started. Otherwise, the scorching pace of growth cannot be achieved—and if achieved, certainly cannot be maintained.

THE ART OF RELINQUISHING CONTROL

Admittedly, it is much easier to slow down and retire for a professional manager, where one is aware of retirement age, right from the start of a career. It is even easier when the corporate policy is defined, and the chairman can hold the position for just five years, irrespective of how outstanding he might have been.

Also, it is easier to let go in the West, than it is to do in the East. The culture is generally different. In the West, entrepreneurs build companies for a sense of achievement and self-satisfaction. In the East, an entrepreneur will keep thinking about building a corporation for his children and his children's children.

In the West, an entrepreneur is more likely to 'wind down' and sell his business, and retire to a place he fancies and can now afford, and travel as much as his health will now permit. In the East, most entrepreneurs will be seen to be steeped in their business till their dying day or till they are incapacitated. They cannot fathom how the business will run without them!

There are exceptions even in the East. There was the gradual pullout by Harish Mahindra, to make way for his young nephew Anand Mahindra, who has carried the group much further from the time he had inherited the empire.

There is the Godrej clan who have been passing on the baton to the next generation in a smooth, planned way for three generations. Godrej group has kept on growing. And some others have managed transitions well and gone riding gracefully into the sunset.

The VUCA world is posing new challenges. Companies, especially in the digitalized world achieve giant size in a short while, and the founder is no longer the undisputed king of all he surveys. Those who invested large sums to make this possible now call the shots. They even pressure the founder to step aside or step down or even step out.

There are cases like Uber in the USA and Housing.com in India. Uber's founder Travis Kalanick was asked to step down after a shareholder revolt made it untenable for him to stay on at the company. Housing.com's co-founder Rahul Yadav was pushed to resign from his CEO post by the board. For gen-next founders, therefore, there is no slow journey towards retirement or even a transfer to professional management. Here is governance, the fourth G of 5Gs!

Many of the start-up founders are young, in their 20s and 30s. There is no question of them providing for their progeny, like in the good old days. There is also the fact that technology is changing so rapidly that the offering of the company may no longer be relevant tomorrow. This would require a massive change, or a sellout or a closure!

Succession planning in a family business will require the kind of knowledge that the founders' children may not be able to provide, and therefore they cannot lead the company. Such a realization has got Bill Gates to retire and hand over the reins to professionally qualified managers who can then provide the vision and the leadership. All this is because of VUCA environment!

Reflection

Many years ago, I had a close friend and mentor, the late Prakash Tandon. He was the first Indian to be appointed chairman of Unilever, India—a singular achievement. This position is always for five years and only for five years. This is irrespective of the brilliance of the person or his great contribution, or his age, which may be much below the retirement age.

Tandon quit before the term was over because he had achieved the goals set. He joined as the chairman of State Trading Corporation of India at the invitation of the then Prime Minister, Indira Gandhi. Again, he quit before the term was over and again for the same reason. Indira Gandhi was upset. She said she had been thinking of a second term for him, but he said that he had done all that he could do and there was no point hanging on. So he went on to be the chairman of the Punjab National Bank and again the same sequence was repeated.

Why do you always do this? I asked him. He said, 'When one attends a dinner party and after dinner, you get up to leave the host will ask to stay back for some more time. You do that and a half hour later when you get up again to leave, the host seems pleased that you are leaving, finally. He thanks and wishes good night. The whole tone changes'

It reminds one of Vijay Merchant, a great Indian cricketer and captain of the team who retired at the height of his career after a test match where he had scored centuries. He was asked by journalists jostling around to interview him:

'Why are you going now, Mr Merchant? Why?'

And Merchant replied, 'I much prefer to be asked why rather than when are you going? That is why I am retiring now'.

It is not easy for entrepreneur-founders of successful corporations to prepare for voluntary retirement. For such entrepreneurs, the business is their love and passion. Their life has been consumed by their business, and they have not had time perhaps for anything else. Not even for leisure or vacations or hobbies. Preparing for retirement, according to experts, begins in childhood with the nurturing of creative and collective hobbies. These hobbies are what one comes back to in retirement. The result: You live your retirement exactly as you have lived your life. With the same concerns and the same values. The only difference is that you disengage from earlier activities and engage in new ones, with different goals but worthy goals nonetheless, as has been done by Bill Gates, and now being followed by Warren Buffett and many others. But many, many more must take this path to find satisfaction for themselves and to make this a better world.

GIVING BACK
To Move Forward

> We have all drunk from wells we did not dig; We have been warmed by fires we did not build; We have sat in the shade of trees we did not plant; We are where we are because of what someone else did.
>
> Author unknown, based on *Deuteronomy 6*

GIVING BACK: THE FIFTH G OF THE 5G SUCCESS FRAMEWORK

In the past, family businesses built up treasure chests over generations. Many among them would donate small or large amounts to aid social and community causes of their interest. A visit to museums and art galleries around the world shows how much wealth the rich and famous families have given in charity, which otherwise they could have kept for themselves and their progeny.

It has been a practice since time immemorial that successful entrepreneurs and business families have shared their affluence with the society to support numerous charitable causes. On the top of this list are education, religion, health, human services, uplifting of underprivileged, environment preservation, arts, culture and humanities. The Rockefeller and Ford Foundations, the Tata Trusts and Birla family Trust, and the Azim Premji Foundation are a few iconic names that get a quick recall. Yet there are hundreds of smaller charitable trusts established by wealthy families and compassionate individuals that are closely connected with local and regional communities. They contribute remarkably in bringing up the standard of living of the community and the society.

Wealth in the world is unevenly divided, and it is a known fact. Oxfam, an international confederation of 20 organizations, working in more than 90 countries to end the injustice that cause poverty, published a report in 2017. The data was startling. It quoted numbers, and the gap between rich and poor across the world. According to the report, *An Economy for the* 99%, India's richest 1% held a huge 58% of the country's total wealth, higher than the global figure of about 50% (*The Hindu* 2017).

According to another *New World Wealth Report*, India was ranked sixth in the list of wealthiest countries, with a total wealth of US$8,230 billion in 2017 and home to 3.3 lakh (0.33 million) high net worth individuals (HNWI). Each of these HNWIs has an individual net assets of US$1 million or more (*GKToday* 2018). These numbers indicate that India is not just keeping pace but is also racing ahead with the wealthy world!

Since the Indian economy has embarked on a path of globalization, wealth has been growing abundantly. Whether new technology start-ups or established business houses run by inheritors and promoter families, enterprising businesses from across industries have benefited from economic reforms. In the VUCA environment, many successful companies have achieved revenues just within a decade, which otherwise, in earlier times, would have taken six to seven decades.

With economic growth, challenges come as a package deal. Preserving the environment and building infrastructure are two prime challenges faced by Indian industries. The new breed of wealthy owners realize that if they are to continue to succeed, they must ensure the social ecosystem of basic amenities and infrastructure is developed and made available to all. They must contribute their wealth for the social causes they believe in and choose to improve.

THE NUEVO TREND

The advent of the 21st century has seen charity activities taking a new shape. Bill Gates and Melinda Gates along with

Warren Buffett have charted a new path for billionaires by pledging to give over half of their wealth to philanthropic causes during their lifetime or after their death (Schwartz 2018). They deserve a big 'thank you' for *The Giving Pledge*, a campaign that is signed by almost 175 billionaires from 22 different countries, as of 2018.

Some of India's later-day billionaires such as Azim Premji, Narayan Murthy, Nandan Nilekani and Shiv Nader have taken similar steps. Having set an example, both of scale and style, they have given a considerable portion of their wealth for philanthropic causes—some earlier, concurrently and later. They have also gone beyond the neighbourhood, even the country, and have adopted the nuevo 'one world' attitude.

It is an example to larger and smaller, all the prosperous businesses that they have an obligation to the community, society and country. Being the 'haves and have-alls', they are expected to help the 'have-nots' to the extent that they feel they can. In a country like India, where the chasm between the rich and the poor is so wide, there is an even more crying need for such an attitude than say in the developed countries with their gender and economic equality, social cohesion and a better work–life balance.

The history of family businesses in India has countless examples of families engaged in charity and philanthropic activities, not because they are socially expected to do so or gain economic advantage, but because 'giving back' to the community and to the society is a sense of gratitude embedded in their genesis. Giving back is one of the five core modules of the success framework for family businesses.

THE SIGNIFICANCE OF GIVING BACK

The concept of charity has evolved with the progress of human civilization. In India, we find charity being a common practice since centuries. Faxian, a Chinese Buddhist monk, studied India by travelling across during the 4th and 5th centuries. He has recorded in his travelogue that there were institutions to take care of the ill and the needy. The affluent merchant families of the *vaishya* community had established houses for dispensing medicine across kingdoms and cities. The poor, destitute and sick were provided with every kind of help such as food, shelter and medications till they got better.

In Richard Stengel's book *Mandela's Way: Lessons for an Uncertain Age*, Nelson Mandela has mentioned in the preface,

> [I]n Africa, there is a concept known as *Ubuntu*— the profound sense that we are human only through the humanity of others; if we are to accomplish something in life, it will in equal measure be due to the work and achievements of others.

Giving back is something we don't discuss often as most of us on this planet earth are focused on the struggle of our daily lives to 'have more'. Still, we are aware and conscious about those around us whose daily meal is barely a piece of bread or a roti. The thought and the act of giving to the lesser privileged has been the hallmark of humanity. There are many reasons which make human beings generous and involve in charity. We find four basic reasons that drive individuals and business families to give back to the society (Khan 2017).

Gives a Sense of Gratitude

We human beings constantly keep 'taking' from the universe, Mother Earth and our fellow humans. The awareness about our obligations makes us thankful for life, health, wealth, career, family, friends, technology and more. Our sense of gratitude helps us realize and appreciate what we have, rather than what we do not have. The mindfulness about what we are grateful for can lessen our tendency to want more to the extent of being greedy.

The Roman politician Cicero has said, 'Gratitude is not only the greatest of virtues but the parent of all others'. Gratitude is recognition of goodness and being thankful. Our beliefs about life as a precious gift, compassion for strangers, kindness towards others and indebtedness towards our loved ones, are directly related to our sense of gratitude.

Many entities invariably contribute in the success of a business venture. Often the entrepreneurs have to 'take first' from stakeholders—who may be customers, employees, banks, institutions, suppliers, vendors and the family. Later in life, when the means and resources are available, to 'give back' is a natural response. Such a sense of obligation is usually one of the success factors for family businesses. Harmony and cohesion in the family, especially among cousins and extended families, remain strong when the sense of gratitude is deeply rooted in the culture of the family and the organization. Gratitude is the glue that keeps generations of the family bonded in spite of adversities and complexities of the environment.

Builds a Culture of Giving

The sense of giving develops as early as the child starts understanding the transactions in the family. Behaviours are contagious. A child learns by watching the behaviour of others. Similarly, when people observe others doing charity or funding a cause, it is likely that they also get motivated. For organizations as well as communities, the culture of 'giving' is inspirational, whether in tangible or intangible form. The inspiration to give back to the community and the society can come from many sources, someone known in the social circle or a role model, or belief in supernatural power, or the surrounding environment. It is the intelligence to contribute and add value to other's life that is meaningful.

For most business communities in India, the culture of giving has its genesis in the religious values. To serve others and to help the needy are the ethos expounded by all the religions, irrespective of regions and nations. This is one of the reasons for which we find charitable trusts providing free food, potable water dispensing machines, shelters, gardens, libraries and religious places of worship. A common practice in family businesses is that women members, the home makers, work for charitable causes funded by their families. The nuance of this practice is deep. Although not contributing directly to the business, women contribute in nurturing family values in younger generations (*Forbes* 2015) and in strengthening the culture of 'giving back' in the family.

A strong belief in giving back to the world has an obvious benefit of helping others, and it is one of the most therapeutic things we can do for ourselves. Ken Blanchard, a well-known American author and management expert, strongly believes in the power of giving back and says, 'my own experience about all the blessings, I have had in my life is that the more I give away, the more that comes back. That is the way life works, and that is the way energy works'.[1]

---

[1]See https://www.brainyquote.com/authors/ken_blanchard, accessed 12 September 2018.

Musings

Soli Godrej, popularly known as S.P. Godrej, was one of the second generation brothers who did not work in the office or factories. He was the face of Godrej company to the outside world. He took care of being in contact with civil and political authorities, with NGOs, with consular corps and with everyone else where interaction was needed with the outside world.

His pet projects were salt pans and mangroves, green spaces and wildlife. At one time, he was the Sheriff of Mumbai, and for many years he was president of the World Wildlife Fund for Nature. The Godrej family donated the land and building for the WWF in Delhi and had the WWF offices at Godrej premises in Mumbai, all for free.

The Godrej family has stood by what they believed in, which is why they command such a high respect in the community.

Provides a Purpose in Life

Mahatma Gandhi used to say, 'The best way to find you is to lose yourself in the service of others'. Helping, caring and considering for others lead to emotional awareness and a sense of 'feel good'. People are bound to experience an increased level of well-being when they are physically involved in the act of 'give back' to the society. Givers on the whole experience a boost in morale, increased feelings of happiness, greater purpose in life and lower stress levels. It may not be possible to make a huge, noticeable difference in the world like Mother Theresa, Alfred Nobel or Mahatma Gandhi made; still, it is possible to get inspired to volunteer for a cause and it is rewarding to see the impact.

Considerable research has been done on the subject, and it confirms that when we have a purpose outside ourselves, it is good for our mental health as well as physical health, longevity and even our genes.[2] The same findings can be applied for family businesses too. When there is a common purpose, a unified vision of the family and the business, it is easier to grow and sustain over a long time span, irrespective of the forces of VUCA environment.

'Giving back' as a purpose for family businesses has several rewards. It can build the respect and reputation of the family in its community and business in its segment. The purpose gives clarity and direction to employees and boosts their morale. Trust and respect are the sure-shot outcomes when the business has a purpose, a sense of giving back to the society.

> 'The purpose of life is not to be happy. It is to be useful, to be honourable, to be compassionate, to have it make some difference that you have lived and lived well'.
>
> **Ralph Waldo Emerson**

Strengthens the Sense of Community

When people choose to give, they unite in the name of a common cause, irrespective of their sects, castes and religions. Initiatives of giving back encourage dialogues between people, communities and nations. It is a key contributing factor in the building blocks for the future development, strengthening communities and building the nation.

A common drive among family businesses and their communities to donate money for good causes is not only to 'give back'

---

[2]See https://www.forbes.com/sites/alicegwalton/2017/07/10/the-science-of-giving-back-how-having-a-purpose-is-good-for-body-and-brain/#56a8ca606146, accessed 13 June 2018.

but also to preserve their culture. Wealthy families from business communities such as Jain, Bhatia, Marwari, Kutchi, Sindhi, Sikh, Chettiar and Shetty are well known for spending their wealth on community welfare. Religious monuments, educational institutes, hospitals and medical facilities are the evidence of the values and beliefs of business families in giving back to the community.

The Founder's Ethos

Late Dr Desh Bandhu Gupta, founder of Lupin Limited, India's third largest pharmaceutical company (by revenues), was a visionary and a philanthropist.

Dr Kamal Sharma, Vice Chairman, Lupin Limited, shared his views on the philosophy of the founder.

'Businesses which succeed with time are those which begin with the philosophy of *making a difference*. It means making a difference to all the stakeholders, be it the shareholders, investors, lenders, employees, customers, suppliers, vendors and the society at large. Each one should get a sense of value-add, though each one will define his value-add in his own way.

If the entrepreneur wants to build a sound and sustainable business, then it must begin with a commitment to making a difference to the society. The reason is that the philosophy underlying the business determines the gene pool of a business. The strategy, the systems, the structures and the style get defined. Making a difference is an ever enduring phenomenon. You never stop making a difference, and as the society keeps expanding, so does your area of influence.

Dr Gupta started Lupin with the manufacture of drugs for tuberculosis (TB) and other infectious diseases in 1968 with a clear purpose of making a difference to the lives of poor people of India. His way of 'giving back' to the society was to provide affordable anti-TB drugs to cure the ailing millions of the debilitating disease. TB was rampant then due to unhygienic living, poor sanitation, water quality and malnutrition in rural India. Drugs from multinationals were expensive. So he decided to provide low cost, good quality medicines for TB. Thereafter, the company expanded into multiple therapy areas and into overseas advanced markets of USA and Japan, but the guiding philosophy remained unchanged'.

According to Dr Sharma,

'The entire business model of Lupin Limited evolved around the philosophy of making a difference. Over a period, we became the prime movers in TB medicines. Our work efficiency, technology and strategies revolved around making high-quality medicines accessible and affordable. Over time, Lupin has acquired global leadership in TB treatment. If you are designing a business model around the thought of making a difference, then it becomes a winning model in the long run.

Today, we are the world's largest suppliers of affordable anti-TB drugs of world-class quality, in addition to other specialties. The company's revenues are approx. $2.5 billion, of which 75% is contributed by overseas markets, the leader being USA with 45% share. I am glad our ethos has prevailed'.

FROM CHARITY TO PHILANTHROPY

The concept and practice of charity in India has been prevalent since the time of the *Rigveda*. Charity or giving is considered a virtue of generosity. It is an action of relinquishing the ownership of what is considered as one's own and giving it to the recipient without expecting anything in return. The act is also known as *daan* in ancient texts of Hinduism. Daan can take the form of feeding a hungry person or giving whatever is required by an individual in stress. In Hindu scriptures, Karna, Mahabali and Harishchandra are the heroes known for 'giving' (Agarwal 2010).

According to Devdutt Pattanaik, author of *Business Sutra*, merchant communities in India (vaishya *varna*) who patronized Buddhist and Jain monks made sense of the world using their sense of profit and loss. Good deeds (*punya*) were seen as earning spiritual profits and bad deeds (*paap*) were seen as earning spiritual losses. Charity and daan were thus considered as the ways of earning good deeds.

The concept of charity is to help people in need through money, medicine and any other physical resource to ease their immediate distress. Philanthropy has an extended connotation. It is a catalytic act that facilitates long-term change for the distressed. Samuel Johnson defined philanthropy as 'love of mankind (humankind); good nature'. There is a degree of overlap in charity and philanthropy, though they are different concepts. Charity aims to relieve the pain of a particular social problem, whereas philanthropy attempts to address the cause of the problem.

The term philanthropist is most often used for those who donate large sums of money or make an impact through a volunteering act. In true sense, a philanthropist is the one who cares for someone else's needs instead of his or her own, by offering personal time, money and other resources to charitable causes. At times we know the causes are unworthy, or the philanthropist has selfish motives like avoiding taxes or gaining popularity.

In the VUCA environment, the world has shrunk and become a global village, thanks to the Internet revolution. The concept of charity has moved to a new dimension of philanthropy. Wealthy, wise and well-known families across the globe follow one common practice—professionally organized philanthropic activities. About 81% of world's richest families practice philanthropy. Their overall interest in philanthropy is indicated not only by their participation but also by their evaluation of the progress of effective giving. Through family foundations, almost 47% of affluent families do philanthropy in an organized and sustained manner (Englisch 2015).

From families, philanthropy has moved to corporates. In India, according to the Companies Act, 2013, corporates of certain size and constitution have to mandatorily get engaged in enlisted projects and programmes related to social welfare and improvement. This concept of corporate social responsibility (CSR) assumes significance as it permits companies to conduct philanthropic activities in a planned, structured and strategic manner by setting up CSR divisions and foundations.

THAT PERSONAL TOUCH

It is so much easier to write a cheque to promote your favourite cause and then shut yourself from the 'milling crowds' that you have tried to help. You can salve your conscience that you have done your bit, and step aside and let the world go on!

It is much more difficult and taxing to get 'personally involved' in the cause, and devote time and effort in the process. When family members, besides being the donors, also become participants in the philanthropic activities, their involvement can create a great impact on the employees and help build the culture of 'giving back'.

Business families usually desire that their businesses last indefinitely. They set up family foundations with the hope that their legacy of charity will be carried forward by future generations. A few succeed and more fail, if the future generations have no interest in the family's charitable work. A family foundation is an effective mechanism to pass the reins of charitable activities which they or their parents founded to their children and grandchildren.

A family foundation is established to meet specific philanthropic goals. Also, the foundation clearly depicts the donor's charitable intent. In addition, a family foundation may serve two unique purposes within the confines of familial walls. A foundation can assist a donor in maintaining the integrity of his or her charitable intent for many years into the future, as well as help to inspire the character, sense of community and love of knowledge of future generations.[3]

The millennial heirs from wealthy families, educated and suave, having a family lineage of capitalism and philanthropy, are managing their family foundations professionally. Whether Justin Rockefeller, the fifth generation heir of the Rockefeller family or Roshini Nader, heading the Shiv Nader Foundation—born out of selling HCL Technologies founded by her father Shiv Nader—these next-gen members devote their expertise,

[3]See https://finconcepts.com/wp-content/uploads/sites/68/2017/04/Assets-Vol-37-No-2.pdf, accessed 13 June 2018.

time and energy in measuring the impact and effectiveness of philanthropy.

Bill and Melinda Gates have set an example. They are fully involved in their philanthropic activities. Maybe they can afford to do so, but they need not have to! They keep trooping across Africa and Asia, physically checking what is being done, how it is being done and what the outcomes are. As a result, they have expanded the causes to focus, which earlier was only HIV. By being deeply involved, they will see more, know more and realign their priorities to get the best 'value for the buck' in philanthropy.

For a Cause

T. Thomas was the chairman of Hindustan Levers in India some years ago, an efficient executive who made a significant contribution to the company. Under his aegis, the company donated one of their warehouses in Mumbai to Mother Theresa for a home so she could accommodate the ill and dying there, and look after them till their last breath. With this act of philanthropy, Thomas did not stop. He worked at the home every Saturday for half a day doing all that needed to be done. It added a new dimension to a person who was known to be 'an iron man'. It showed that he had also given his heart, apart from the money and place from the company, to Mother Theresa's charities.

Walter Saldanha, a doyen of the advertising industry, pioneered the start-up of Chaitra Advertising in Mumbai in 1972, Later it became Leo-Burnett, one of the top adverting agencies of India. Walter involved himself with Shanti Avedna, the hospice for dying cancer patients in Bandra in Mumbai. It was not surprising to find Walter every evening at the reception counter, attending to administrative work at Shanti Avedna.

He went beyond just donating money. He became a part of the project with the limited time that he could spare.

These lesser-known heroes and their commitment to the cause of giving back make our lives enriched. As Denzel Washington, the Hollywood movie star says, 'at the end of the day, it's not about what you have or even what you've accomplished. It is about who you've lifted up. Who you've made better. It's about what you've given back'.

INDIA: THE EMERGING LANDSCAPE OF PHILANTHROPY

The Oxfam report[4] mentioned that since 2015, the richest 1% of the world had owned more wealth than the rest of the planet. Globally, just eight billionaires have the same amount of wealth as the poorest 50% of the world population. The study said there are 84 billionaires in India, with a collective wealth of $248 billion, led by Mukesh Ambani ($19.3 billion), Dilip Shanghvi ($16.7 billion) and Azim Premji ($15 billion). The total Indian wealth in the country stood at $3.1 trillion.[5]

In January 2018, another Oxfam report, titled *Reward Work, Not Wealth* revealed how the global economy enables the wealthy elite to accumulate vast wealth, even as hundreds of millions of people struggle to survive on poverty pay. It also said India's top 10% of the population holds 73% of the wealth, and 37% of India's billionaires have inherited family wealth. They control 51% of the total wealth of billionaires in the country (*The Times of India* 2018).

---

[4]See https://www.oxfam.org/en/pressroom/pressreleases/2015-01-19/richest-1-will-own-more-all-rest-2016, accessed 13 June 2018.
[5]See http://www.thehindu.com/business/Economy/Richest-1-own-58-of-total-wealth-in-India-Oxfam/article17044486.ece, accessed 13 June 2018.

FIGURE 5.1 INDIA'S WEALTH PYRAMID

92% of Indian adults have wealth of less than $10,000

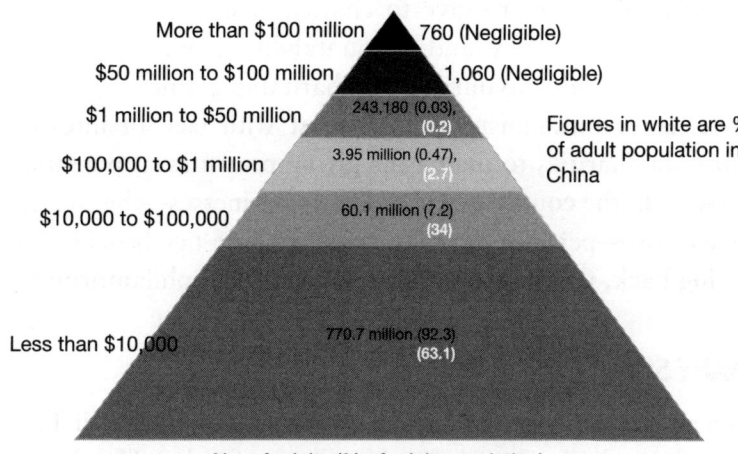

More than $100 million — 760 (Negligible)

$50 million to $100 million — 1,060 (Negligible)

$1 million to $50 million — 243,180 (0.03), (0.2)

$100,000 to $1 million — 3.95 million (0.47), (2.7)

$10,000 to $100,000 — 60.1 million (7.2) (34)

Less than $10,000 — 770.7 million (92.3) (63.1)

Figures in white are % of adult population in China

No. of adults (% of adult population)

All adults with wealth above $1 million

Source: Credit Suisse (2017); courtesy graphic by Subrata Jana/*Mint*

India's wealth pyramid (Figure 5.1) shows that at the bottom, 92.3% of adults have wealth less than $10,000. Above them are 7.2% adults in the $10,000 to $100,000 bracket and 0.5% of Indian have wealth over $100,000. Only about 0.03% of Indians have wealth more than $1 million.

The landscape of philanthropy in India is changing. Many multi-generational business families in a grand scale philanthropy are going through succession transition. The choices, decisions and responsibilities of philanthropy activities are transitioning from the incumbent generation to the next generation. The Oxfam report mentions that over the next 20 years, 500 people will hand over $2.1 trillion to their heirs—a sum larger than the GDP of India, a country of 1.3 billion people. According to a Karvy Private Wealth (2017) report, India will witness one of the largest transfers of wealth—close to $128 billion—from one generation to the next in the coming decade.

A crucial factor in promoting philanthropy is the government's policies. The Bain report suggests reasons why Indians might be reluctant to give to charity. There is a perceived lack of transparency and accountability among charities; tax laws are not favourable to charitable giving. Also, the governance mechanism is not robust with lack of information on charities to match the giving priorities of potential donors. In the countries where family businesses—the wealth generators—perceive that the laws promote tax benefits for giving back, they are more likely to engage in philanthropy.

MANY SHADES OF GIVING

Giving has many shades. There are those like Jamshedji Tata for whom the business was always a profit plus. He always tried to align the business to a larger purpose. To make steel was to help India to be an industrial nation. It meant locating iron ore and coal preferably close to each other, and building a whole infrastructure from the ground up. The result: Jamshedpur, as we know it today. Again, the dream of making automobiles, an extension of the steel business, led to TISCO and TELCO, and later Tata Power and TOMCO. All of them became giants of Indian industry. He always looked around to see what was missing and what would help the country.

Jamshedji Tata was able to envision and then fund organizations like the Tata Institute of Social Sciences. His successors then following through with institutions such as the Tata Institute of Fundamental Research, Tata Cancer Hospital and National Centre for Performing Arts.

Giving was ingrained in the organization. Even professional managers later developed an attitude and way of thinking which was pioneering, especially in the early 1900s in India.

Akin to the Tatas, there is a class of family businesses which are influenced and conditioned by the environment in which they operate. In turn, they try to influence the environment. A textile mill in Navsari, an engineering company in Kolhapur, an aluminium plant in Renukoot—these businesses have the pull of serving the poor and the illiterate in the villages all around them. They embark on starting schools, and sometimes colleges or skill development institutes to prepare the natives for employment. They help in improving water supply by digging wells or organizing irrigation. Their philanthropy is in improving the standard of living, not just in the manufacturing town but also in the neighbourhood locality. The operations hub of the family business becomes the centre from which the spokes, the deeds of 'giving back' emanate in different directions.

Musings

The ingrained attitude is evident in a story told about Russi Modi, the chief of TISCO during the Licence Raj era of the 1970s and 1980s. The labour union representatives had complained about the state of the toilets in the plant. Modi asked the personnel head to attend to the complaint and also asked him how long it would take to correct the situation. The personnel head gave about two months' time estimate. Modi felt it was unreasonable. So he instructed that the 'officers toilet' signboard be put outside the worker's toilets and vice versa.

Result: the worker's toilets were brought up to form in just one week. The signboards were then changed again! Here was a form of philanthropy within the company rather than the outside.

One more shade of giving is connected with the donor family's personal calamity. If one or more family members are affected by any misfortune, then the family donates for that cause. If a young man dies of cancer, then the family becomes a staunch supporter of the Cancer Aid Society. It is the thought process, 'we could not save our son. Let us now try and save others from this disease'.

Hong Kong's richest man, Li Ka-shing, also been referred to as Asia's answer to Warren Buffett, brought down the curtain on his rag to riches career on 10 May 2018, saying 'he had done the best he could have done'. According to *Forbes* magazine, Li Ka-shing's assets are estimated to be $33.3 billion. He passed on the reins to his son Victor. Li said that he plans to spend his time and focus on charity, the Li Ka Shing Foundation to which he has already pledged a third of his assets. This foundation funds education and health initiatives throughout the world.

EDUCATION: THE PHILANTHROPIC APPROACH

There are family businesses in India that have set up educational institutes named after the founder and the family. The Birla family is renowned for philanthropy in education, for building world-class institutes such as the Birla Institute of Technology and Science in their hometown Pilani in Rajasthan. Birla schools are present in almost all the major cities of India. Likewise, several other families have set up secondary and higher education schools. Prominent business families such as Bajaj, Ruia, Ruparel, Poddar, Somaiya, Narsee Monjee, Munjal and T.M.A. Pai have contributed to establish top-notch education institutes. The philanthropic approach is towards building capabilities through education of people who cannot afford.

In last few decades, foreign education has become accessible and affordable to India's rich and upper-middle class.

World-class universities in the USA and in European countries attract a large quantum of students. The younger generation of wealthy and prosperous business families attend prestigious institutes abroad. There is also a spurt in donations to the alma mater by these students. It is to support the institute as well as to say 'thank you' for all the grooming and development that has been done for them. It also helps to put the family name on the exclusive board listing out the donors.

Indian alma maters have not lagged behind. In recent years, there have been substantial donations to top-notch education institutes in India. IIT Bombay stands tall when it comes to eminent alumni. Over the last 15 years, IIT Bombay alumni across the world have contributed an estimated ₹2 billion for their alma mater, and continue to do so in an engaging and innovative manner (India Infoline 2011).

Musings

There is the story of Mr and Mrs Stanford, who went to see the dean of Harvard Business School because their son who was studying at Harvard had died in an accident. They wanted to donate to set up an institute in his memory. The dean kept this old, simply dressed couple waiting a long time, and then took them to the window of his office. Pointing to a building, he said that such a building would cost some millions. And implying—can they really afford it?

Mr and Mrs Stanford felt insulted. The dean had been misled by their simple attire and quiet demeanour. They both went back to California, and instead of donating to Harvard, put in some more money and started Stanford University, no less than a staunch competitor to Harvard!

SERVING OTHERS, SERVING THE SELF

There are business families who combine philanthropy with promoting their family name or corporate identity, preferring media attention by indirectly announcing their philanthropic activities, not just a pure act of benevolence. If one walks around any city in India, benches at public places, drinking water taps and dispensers are found with the names of donors prominently displayed on them. There are also family businesses which start out a charity venture to help the poor— perhaps a hospital or a school. And over time, the venture grows to become a reputed and profitable institution. It then ceases to be a charity and becomes one more business unit to the family business when it was never originally intended to be!

There are always whispers that family trusts are used by family businesses to divert funds to create tax-free income. It is the governance challenge and blatantly erroneous. It may be an incorrect and biased view to paint every philanthropic trust with the same brush. Most of those who involve themselves in philanthropy do it with their mind, heart and soul, and they are the ones who help to make this a better world.

THE GIVERS OF INDIA

In the early days of industrialization under the British Raj, philanthropy was limited to the initiatives undertaken by benevolent zamindars (land owners) and rich traders. During the independence movement, several industrialists extended their financial support to leaders of the freedom struggle. G.D. Birla's financial contributions to the movement and Ardeshir Godrej's generous donation to the Tilak Fund for the upliftment of Harijans (untouchables) were notable among these. The Tata and the Murugappa families pioneered charitable contributions to hospitals and schools.

Creating townships as a means to promote employee welfare was among India's primary tenets of corporate philanthropy in post-Independence era. 'In a free enterprise', said Jamshedji Tata, 'the community is not just another stakeholder in business but is, in fact, the very purpose of its existence'.[6] Carrying forward the legacy, Ratan Tata wrote in the *Code of Honor*, a book on the Tata group's attitude to CSR, 'we have to grasp the imperative of putting back into the community from which we gain as a corporate'.

'The desire for an altruistic connection to humanity is something we all carry', says Marguerite Griffin, Northern Trust's national director of philanthropic devices.

> It's easy to get caught in the technical aspects of charitable giving—what vehicle to use or who are going to be involved—but it's so important to identify why you're doing it and what you want to accomplish. There's a personal side of giving that needs to be addressed.[7]

The act of philanthropy has become focused, structured and strategic in last few decades. A trend is visible where more and more families are institutionalizing their philanthropic activities in the form of trust funds or foundations. Funds contributed by individual philanthropists have been steadily rising, growing faster than funds from foreign sources and funds contributed through CSR. Philanthropists are also becoming more sophisticated in how they view giving and are

---

[6]'Temples, Townships and Schools: India's Philanthropic Legacy', 19 May 2011. http://knowledge.wharton.upenn.edu/article/temples-townships-and-schools-indias-philanthropic-legacy/, accessed 12 September 2018.
[7]See https://wealth.northerntrust.com/wealth-management/the-hidden-benefits-of-giving-back, accessed 12 September 2018.

proactively adopting new strategies to move the needle towards high-impact results.

The philanthropy arena in India is still emerging and facing challenges, unlike the long history of structured philanthropy in developed countries. The latent potential of India, an emerging economy of more than a billion people, continues to be stymied by developmental barriers. India's development goals are immense and the challenges that lie ahead can only overcome with the efforts of every stakeholder in the ecosystem. The role of the individual philanthropist in overcoming these goals is critical (Sheth, Sanghavi, Bhagwati, Srinivasan and Dastoor 2017).

According to the *India Philanthropy Report* (2017) by Bain & Company and Dasra, a non-government organization (NGO), the number of UHNWI households has more than doubled to 146,000 in the year 2016 from 62,000 in the year 2011.

India's top industrialists, entrepreneurs and CEOs have been donating millions for humanitarian causes. According to the Huran India Philanthropy list 2015 (Bhattacharya 2016), Azim Premji, Wipro chief and IT tycoon, was the most generous Indian of the year who donated ₹275 billion for education (Figure 5.2). It is not just the act of philanthropy; it is the belief system of the donors that make them exceptional and admirable. Azim Premji has said, 'I strongly believe that those of us, who are privileged to have wealth, should contribute significantly to try and create a better world for the millions who are far less privileged'.

These philanthropists have been giving away a significant portion of their wealth for causes such as education, women empowerment, social and rural development, health, sanitation, environment preservation and entrepreneurship (*Firstpost* 2015).

FIGURE 5.2 TOP 10 PHILANTHROPISTS OF 2015

The Hurun India Philanthropy List 2015 saw 36 philanthropists give more than 10 crore. Education remains the most favoured philanthropic cause, accounting for 84% of donations.

● Rank ■ Donation in ₹ crore

Azim Premji
■ 27,514

Nandan and Rohini Nilekani
■ 2,404

N.R. Narayana Murthy
■ 1,322

K. Dinesh and family
■ 1,238

Shiv Nadar
■ 535

Mukesh Ambani
■ 345

Sunny Varkey and family
■ 326

Ronnie Screwvala
■ 158

Rahul Bajaj and family
■ 139

Pallonji Mistry
■ 96

↑ Increase in Rankings ◆Retained Ranking
↓ Down compared with last year

Source: Hurun India Philanthropy List 2015

The philanthropy scenario is definitely changing. According to Hurun India Rich List 2017, there are 617 individuals with a cut-off of ₹10 billion, compared to 339 in 2016. There are 300% more women in the list compared to that of 2016, and the number of self-made women have increased from two to eight (Hurun.net 2017).

The global business environment and stakeholders' growing expectations have encouraged businesses to pay close attention not only to their philanthropic activities but also to the measurable social impact of these activities. Companies view their philanthropic programmes not only as corporate or family resources meant for social development but also as strategic social investments intended to achieve measurable outcomes and impacts. Corporate philanthropy programmes are often a part of the organization's mission, and are designed to address social and political issues that affect the business.

MILLENNIAL PHILANTHROPISTS

Facebook founder Mark Zuckerberg and his wife Dr Priscilla Chan's creation of the Chan Zuckerberg Initiative is a philanthropic organization to which they have pledged 99% of their Facebook shares. Epitomes of such generosity are rising in the younger generations, and such instances demonstrate that the rich on the philanthropic route are not seeking good public relations from their altruistic behaviour, but rather see giving as an opportunity for meaningful work.

The Millennial Impact Report released by the Case Foundation looks at philanthropic trends among millennials in Asia. It surveyed a sample of 2,265 millennials. According to the report, 83% of millennials made a financial donation to at least one non-profit, which puts their giving on levels comparable to American households as a whole. About 73% of the millennials surveyed said that they gave their time to a non-profit organization in the past year, almost triple the rate of volunteerism among the greater American population. About 70% said they were willing to fundraise for causes they cared for. This is the level of engagement of the new generation of donors who are open to sustained funding and becoming evangelists of organizations (Ton 2013).

Many multi-generational philanthropic families are at a stage of transition of leadership and succession from one generation to the next. For such transitions, philanthropic activities in the form of family foundations serve as excellent forums for family collaboration and a means of transferring the mantle of philanthropic stewardship to succeeding generations.

Reflexions: Giving Back

India is not only among the countries with the highest concentration of wealth in the richest 1% of the population but also among the countries where this concentration has increased most sharply since the year 2000. The same situation is in China, where the wealth is increasingly cornered by the top end of the pyramid. The increase in China has been 18%, and in India, it is 12%.

There are people who believe that the disadvantaged ones are where they are because of their deeds of an earlier life, and they are now paying for their sins. If they make sufficient amends, then they will come back again into this life as part of the 'haves'. Such believers may avoid feeling guilty and console themselves so that it becomes easy to live life without pangs of conscience.

Mahatma Gandhi kept repeating that the wealth of the rich is not their wealth, but that they are 'trustees' of the wealth, on behalf of all humanity. This wealth is to be used for the public good so that it is spread around to make as many people healthy and happy as is possible. Similar was the philosophy of the early pioneers like Jamshedji Tata. The Tata trusts are today among the largest contributors of charity in the country. The group is among the largest conglomerates, but Tata is still not among the top 10 richest men in India.

It is the story of the Dead Sea, which is really a lake not a sea. It is so high in salt content that the human body can float on it easily. The salt in the Dead Sea is as high as 35%, which is almost 10 times the amount of salt in the normal ocean water. And with such saltiness, there is no life at all in the Dead Sea. No fish, no vegetation no sea animals. Nothing. And so the name—Dead Sea.

The other sea is the Sea of Galilee, which is just north of the Dead Sea. Both the Seas receive their water from the River Jordan. And yet they are both extremely different. The Sea of Galilee is pretty and resplendent with a rich and colourful marine life. There are lots of plants and it is home to 20 different types of fishes. The same region and the same source of water, and yet one sea is dead and the other is full of life. Why is this?

The River Jordan flows into the Sea of Galilee and then flows out. The water simply passes through the Sea of Galilee, in and then out, and that keeps the sea healthy and vibrant, and teeming with marine life. But the Dead Sea is so far below the mean sea level that it has no outlet. The water flows in, but does not flow out. It is estimated that several million tons of water evaporates from the Dead Sea every day, leaving it salty—too full of minerals and unfit for any marine life.

The Dead Sea takes water from the River Jordan and holds it. It does not give.

The result? No life at all!

Life is not about just getting. It is also about giving. We all need to be like the Sea of Galilee.

We are fortunate to get wealth, knowledge, love and respect. But if we don't learn to give, we could all end up like the Dead Sea. If we get the Dead Sea mentality of merely taking in more water, more money and more everything, the results can be disastrous!

'Giving back' completes the 5G success framework for a family business in a VUCA world and leaves us with a thought: *You get a living with what you earn, and you get a life by what you give.*

'Kindness in words creates confidence,
Kindness in thinking creates profoundness,
Kindness in giving creates love'.

Lao Tzu, 6 BC

CONCLUSION: THE LAST WORD

Family business will continue to be the bedrock of economic activity in every nation of the world. It will always be the starting point—the first *cell*.

That is why, just like in earlier centuries, in the 21st century also, India's family business domain continues to be the biggest contributor to GDP, the biggest segment of international trade, the biggest employer, and with largest number of units, the biggest asset creator.

Nearly all family businesses follow a life cycle—it starts with the individual, then the family, then a corporation and then a transformation to a new avatar or the death—soon, later or much later.

In a VUCA world, many family businesses grow rapidly and sometimes grow beyond the control of the founder, often in financial terms and sometimes also in management terms.

This is the reason joint family owned businesses are slowly becoming extinct in India, changing the centuries-old norm.

It is interesting to see that the world's largest companies by market valuation, in 2017, were:

Apple	$873 billion
Alphabet	$714 billion
Microsoft	$635 billion
Amazon	$544 billion
Facebook	$520 billion

All these companies have been started by individuals, alone or with partners in the millennial era! A family business is always started by Achievers, who are few in any community. They provide support to the Sustainers who are many. The Achiever entrepreneurs have two traits—Absorption and Agility—in addition to technical or domain skills. They are Passionals—not just Professionals. Tata, FedEx, Walt Disney, Merck and many others were built this way.

Those who graduated from the small family business to the large-sized corporates like Unilever are those who could balance the family system with the business system. Emotional concerns are balanced by business performance. Family needs are balanced by business demands. Maintaining stability is balanced by managing change.

The successful companies have been able to master and manage five pivotal variables: *control* in both ownership and management; *careers*, with regard to the roles of family members and outside professionals in business; *capital*, so they can move ahead; *conflict*, which can be due to the crossing of personal aspirations and business expectations; and *culture*, where business culture must be combined with family values.

If all this is done well and the family business is able to use professionals to its advantage, then the business can achieve great heights. There are inherent advantages that smaller family business has against large, non-family owned business such as:

- Ability to handle workforce better
- Flexibility, with less red tape
- Faster decision-making
- Adaptability in a fast-changing environment

Family business has the advantages of greater commitment and of continuity, which can be seldom replicated in a non-family business.

There are, of course, the disadvantages of lower access to capital, lower access to top management talent because of fears of a glass ceiling, and less innovation. There are many business houses such as Tata, Aditya Birla, Murugappa and Mahindra who have overcome these disadvantages by:

- Separating family interest from company interest
- Creating an environment to recruit and retain outside talent
- Bringing focus to their operations
- Using joint ventures to upgrade their skills
- Following a consistent strategy

While the joint family business is diminishing, families using the 5Gs framework are growing in number. Gone are the days of 1990s when 15 out of the 20 largest industrial houses were run by the trading community referred to as 'Bania'. Eight of whom were Marwaris (hailing from Marwar, a region in west Rajasthan). The base has become much wider. India now has the fourth largest billionaire population in the world (119), with a net worth of $440 billion, as compared to USA (585) with $3,096 billion and China (373) with $1,120 billion.

Nearly all of them are start-up entrepreneurs. Yet they have built businesses of a size way beyond most who have been around for four to five generations. And this is in 2018!

There is still place for family business. But the speed has changed to 5G. The world has changed to VUCA.

Businesses will be started by innovators and dreamers. They will build businesses of valuation size unimaginable a few decades later. They will perhaps not even think of inheritance and passing the business to future generations. Many will give away much of their wealth for the good of the community. They will build and they will move on. And the world will still be a better place because of their contribution. Family business will then also be the foundation of the economic pyramid that we need to build in India and also in most other parts of the world!

REFERENCES

Agarwal, Sanjay. 2010. *DAAN and Other Giving Traditions in India*. New Delhi: MLBD.

Aronoff, Craig, and John Ward. 1994. *How to Choose and Use Advisors: Getting the Best Professional Family Business Advice*. New York, NY: Palgrave Macmillan.

Baermar, Drake. 2015. 'The Secretive Cargill Family Has 14 Billionaires Thanks to an Agricultural Empire—More Than Any Other Clan on Earth'. *Business Insider India*, 3 March.

Balasubramanyam, K.R. 2011. 'Pump and Show'. *Business Today*, 10 July. Available at: https://www.businesstoday.in/magazine/cover-story/kirloskar-brothers-is-122-year-old-company/story/16480.html (Accessed 6 June 2018).

Bertrand, Marianne, and Antoinette Schoar. 2006. 'The Role of Family in Family Firms'. *Journal of Economic Perspectives*, 20 (2, Spring), 73–96.

Bhattacharya, Saumya. 2016. 'Azim Premji the "Most Generous Indian" in Hurun India Philanthropy List 2015'. *Economic Times*, 9 January. Available at: https://economictimes.indiatimes.com/news/company/corporate-trends/azim-premji-the-most-generous-indian-in-hurun-india-philanthropy-list-2015/articleshow/50495746.cms (Accessed 13 June 2018).

Business Today. 2011. '100 Years Young'. *Business Today*, 10 July. Available at: https://www.businesstoday.in/magazine/cover-story/companies-that-have-completed-100-years-in-india/story/16503.html (Accessed 19 July 2018).

Cohen, Allan, and Pramodita Sharma. 2016. *Entrepreneurs in Every Generation*. Oakland, CA: Berrett-Koehler Publishers, Inc.

Credit Suisse. 2017. *Global Wealth Report 2017: Where Are We Ten Years after the Crisis?* 14 November. Available at: https://www.credit-suisse.com/corporate/en/articles/news-and-expertise/global-wealth-report-2017-201711.html (Accessed 13 June 2018).

Cruz, Elfren S. 2016. 'Power of Families' (BREAKTHROUGH). The Philippine Star, 20 October. Available at: https://www.philstar.com/opinion/2016/10/20/1635186/power-families#IFQP4irVetI85O1j.99 (Accessed 25 June 2018).

Das, G. 1999. 'Indian Business Families'. In *Seminar: Special Issue on Family Business—A Symposium on the Role of the Family in Indian Business*, Issue 482. Available at: www.india-seminar.com (Accessed 6 June 2018).

de Geus, Arie. 1997, March/April. 'The Living Company'. Available at: https://hbr.org/1997/03/the-living-company (Accessed 19 June 2018).

Dixit, Mita. 2010. 'Conflict and Splits in Multigenerational Family Owned and Managed Businesses in India'. Unpublished doctoral thesis.

Dixit, Mita. 2015. '3 Ways to Succession Planning for Family Businesses'. *Franchise India*, 27 February. Available at: https://www.franchiseindia.com/entrepreneur/article/managing-a-business/hr/3-ways-to-succession-planning-for-family-businesses-597 (Accessed 19 June 2018).

———. 2016, April. 'Family Governance—The Path of Progress for Indian Family Businesses'. *Maharashtra Chamber Patrika*, xxxxvii (1), 8.

Donnelly, R.G. 1964. 'The Family Business'. *Harvard Business Review*, 42 (4), 93–105.

Dun & Bradstreet. 1973. *The Business Failure Record: 1972*. New York, NY: Dun & Bradstreet.

Dutta, S. 1997. *Family Business in India*. New Delhi: SAGE.

Economist. 2015. 'Family Companies—To Have and to Hold'. *Economist*, special report, 18 April.

Englisch, Peter. 2015. 'Why Philanthropy Is Essential to Family Businesses'. *Forbes*, 1 May. Available at: https://www.forbes.com/sites/ey/2015/05/01/why-philanthropy-is-essential-to-family-businesses/#754016471a91 (Accessed 13 June 2018).

Entrepreneur. 2013. 'Are Entrepreneurs Born or Made?' *Entrepreneur*, October 2013. Available at: https://www.entrepreneur.com/article/228273 (Accessed 6 June 2018).

FICCI. 1999. *Footprints of Enterprise—Indian Business Through the Ages*. Oxford: Oxford University Press.

Firstpost. 2015. 'Infographic: Azim Premji Leads List of Top 10 Indian Philanthropists'. *Firstpost*, 7 July. Available at: https://www.firstpost.com/business/infographic-azim-premji-leads-list-of-top-10-indian-philanthropists-2331572.html (Accessed 13 June 2018).

Forbes. 2015. 'Why Philanthropy Is Essential to Family Businesses'. *Forbes*, 1 May. Available at: https://www.forbes.com/sites/ey/2015/05/01/why-philanthropy-is-essential-to-family-businesses/#54255f501a91 (Accessed 13 June 2018).

Gersick, K.E., J.A. Davis, M.M. Hampton and I. Lansberg. 1997. *Generation to Generation: Life Cycles of the Family Business*. Boston, MA: Harvard Business School Press.

GKToday. 2018. 'India 6th Wealthiest Country: New World Wealth Report'. GKToday, 31 January. Available at: https://currentaffairs.gktoday.in/india-6th-wealthiest-country-world-wealth-report-01201852121.html (Accessed 13 June 2018).

Haber, Jason. 2016. 'Why Millennials May Just Be the Best Entrepreneurial Generation Ever'. *Entrepreneur India*, May 2016. Available at: https://bebusinessed.com/history/history-of-entrepreneurship/ (Accessed 6 June 2018).

Hall, Alan. 2012. 'To Succeed as an Entrepreneur, Know Your Customer'. *Forbes Entrepreneur*, 14 June.

Hurun.net. 2017. 'Hurun Report Releases Hurun India Rich List 2017'. Hurun Research. 26 September. Available at: http://www.hurun.net/EN/Article/Details?num=1F570C35BCA2 (Accessed 13 June 2018).

Heitzman, Adam. 2015. How Entrepreneurship Might Be Genetic'. *Inc.com*, 27 January. Available at: https://www.inc.com/adam-heitzman/how-entrepreneurship-might-be-genetic.html (Accessed 6 June 2018).

India Infoline. 2011. 'IIT Bombay Alumni Gives ₹2bn to Alma Mater'. India Infoline News Service, Mumbai, 18 August. Available at: https://www.indiainfoline. com/article/news/iit-bombay-alumni-gives-rs-2bn-to-alma-mater-5224355290_1. html (Accessed 13 June 2018).

Karvy Private Wealth. 2017. *India Wealth Report 2017.* Available at: http://www. karvywealth.com/india-wealth-report-2017/ (Accessed 13 June 2018).

Khan, Laeeka. 2017.10 Reasons Why Giving Back to Society Is Important. 17 July. Available at: https://www.lyceum.co.za/press-releases/10-reasons-why-giving-back-to-society-is-important (Accessed 13 June 2018).

Koeberle-Schmid, A., Denise Kenyon-Rouvinez and Ernesto J. Poza. 2014. *Governance in Family Enterprise.* New York, NY: Palgrave Macmilan.

Lamont, James. 2010. 'Indian Groups Failing to Plan for Successor'. *Financial Times,* 6 August. Available at: https://www.ft.com/content/32b3c25a-a175-11df-9656-00144feabdc0 (Accessed 19 June 2018).

Leach, Peter. 2007. *Family Businesses—The Essentials.* UK: Profile Books Ltd.

Leenders M., and E. Waarts. 2003. 'Competitiveness and Evolution of Family Businesses: The Role of Family and Business Orientation'. *European Management Journal,* 21 (6), 686–697.

Mathur, Nandita. 2016. 'Only 15% of Indian Family Businesses Have Robust Succession Plan: PwC Report'. *LiveMint,* 22 November. Available at: https://www.livemint.com/Politics/u3sNtNjbcq98ls9ClG7vTP/Family-businesses-have-contributed-to-growth-of-every-sector.html (Accessed 19 June 2018).

McIntyre, Douglas A., Alexander E.M. Hess and Samuel Weigley. 2013. 'Eight Founders Who Ruined Their Companies'. *USA Today,* 10 February. Available at: https://www.usatoday.com/story/money/business/2013/02/09/founders-ruin-companies/1905921/ (Accessed 6 June 2018).

Mukherji, Rahul. 2009. 'The State, Economic Growth, and Development in India'. *India Review,* 8 (1), 81–106.

Myers, Joe. 2016. 'India's Astonishing Start-up Boom—All You Need to Know in 5 Charts'. *World Economic Forum,* 3 October. Available at: https://www.weforum. org/agenda/2016/10/india-startup-boom-in-charts/ (Accessed 6 June 2018).

Naidu, Viren. 2014. 'Are Our CEOs VUCA-ready?' *The Economic Times,* 23 September.

O'Connell, Ainsley. 2014. 'How the Word "Entrepreneur" Got Too Popular for Its Own Good?' *Fast Company,* 4 April. Available at: https://www.fastcompany. com/3029196/how-the-word-entrepreneur-got-too-popular-for-its-own-good (Accessed 6 June 2018).

Pande, Shamni. 2011. 'Growth Tonic'. *Business Today,* 10 July.

Piramal, G. 1999. 'Big Business and Entrepreneurship'. In *Seminar: Special Issue on Family Business—A Symposium on the Role of the Family in Indian Business.* Available at: www.india-seminar.com (Accessed 6 June 2018).

PwC. 2016. *The Family Business Sector in 2016: Success and Succession.* Available at: https://www.pwc.com/gx/en/services/family-business/family-business-survey-2016/ succession.html (Accessed 19 June 2018).

PwC. 2016. *PwC India Family Business Survey 2016: Aligning with India's Growth Story*. Available at: https://www.pwc.in/assets/pdfs/publications/family-business-survey-2016/pwc-india-family-business-survey-2016-aligning-with-indias-growth-story.pdf (Accessed 19 June 2018).

Rediff.com. 2016. 'In India, 15 of the Top 20 Business Groups Are Family-owned!' 18 August. Available at: http://www.rediff.com/money/report/special-in-india-15-of-the-top-20-business-groups-are-family-owned/20160818.htm (Accessed 19 June 2018).

Reid, Renee. 1999. 'Family Orientation in Family Firms: A Model and Some Empirical Evidence'. *Journal of Small Business and Enterprise Development*, 6 (1), 55–67.

Sagar, Neeraj, and Rajeev Vasudeva. 2017. 'Each Succeeding Generation Sees the Family Business Not as a Matter of Ownership, But of Trusteeship'. Available at: https://www.egonzehnder.com/insight/each-succeeding-generation-sees-the-family-business-not-as-a-matter-of-ownership-but-of-trusteeship (Accessed 25 June 2018).

Sampath, D. 2001. *Inheriting the Mantle: Management of Succession and Transition in Indian Family Businesses*. New Delhi: SAGE.

Scheele, Adele M. 2004, July. 'An Anatomy of Success: Proven Action Steps That Lead to Achievement'. *Journal of Dental Education*, 68 (7), 47–51.

Schwantes, Marcel. 2018. 'Principal and Founder, Leadership From the Core'. Available at: https://www.inc.com/marcel-schwantes/warren-buffet-says-you-should-hire-people-based-on-these-3-traits-but-only-1-truly-matters.html

Schwartz, Ariel. 2018. 'Bill Gates Reveals the 2 Reasons Why He's Giving Away His $90 Billion Fortune'. *Business Insider*, 13 February.

Sheth, Arpan, Deval Sanghavi, Anant Bhagwati, Srikrishnan Srinivasan and Pakistan Dastoor. 2017, 4 March. *India Philanthropy Report 2017*. Available at: http://www.bain.com/publications/articles/india-philanthropy-report-2017.aspx (Accessed 13 June 2018).

Sull, Donald. 2009, February. 'How to Thrive in Turbulent Markets'. Available at: https://hbr.org/2009/02/how-to-thrive-in-turbulent-markets (Accessed 19 June 2018).

Tagiuri, Renato, and John Davis. 1996. 'Bivalent Attributes of the Family Firms'. *Family Business Review*, 9 (2), 199–208.

The Guardian. 2000. 'The Fall and Rise of the Gucci Empire'. *The Guardian*, 3 October. Available at: https://www.theguardian.com/g2/story/0,3604,376489,00.html (Accessed 19 June 2018).

Tharawat Magazine. 2010. 'Inside the SPARK Succession Program: Interview with Abdullah Ali Almajdouie'. *Tharawat Magazine*, 1 July. Available at: https://www.tharawat-magazine.com/family-business-succession/spark-succession-program-almajdouie/#gs.xYZhmrM (Accessed 19 July 2018).

———. 2013. 'The Family Business Life Cycle'. *Tharawat Magazine*, 3 July. Available at: https://www.tharawat-magazine.com/family-business-succession/family-business-life-cycle/#gs.IIV1kXc (Accessed 19 June 2018).

The Hindu. 2017. 'Richest 1% Own 58% of Total Wealth in India: Oxfam'. *The Hindu*, 16 January, Davos. Available at: http://www.thehindu.com/business/Economy/

Richest-1-own-58-of-total-wealth-in-India-Oxfam/article17044486.ece (Accessed 13 June 2018).

The Times of India. 2018. 'India's Richest 1% Corner 73% of Wealth Generation: Survey'. *The Times of India*, 22 January. Available at: https://timesofindia.indiatimes.com/business/india-business/indias-richest-1-corner-73-of-wealth-generation-survey/articleshow/62598222.cms (Accessed 13 June 2018).

Ton, Anh. 2013. 'How Millennials Do Philanthropy'. *Asian Philanthropy Forum*, 13 August. Available at: http://www.asianphilanthropyforum.org/millennial-philanthropy/ (Accessed 13 June 2018).

Tripathi, D. 1992. 'Indian Business Houses and Entrepreneurship: A Note on Research Trends'. *Journal of Entrepreneurship*, 1 (1), 75–97.

———. 1999. 'Change and Continuity'. In *Seminar: Special Issue on Family Business—A Symposium on the Role of the Family in Indian Business*, Issue 482. Available at: www.india-seminar.com (Accessed 6 June 2018).

Unnikrishnan, C.H. 2016. 'Family Businesses: Winds of Change'. *Business World*, 28 December. Available at: http://businessworld.in/article/Family-Businesses-Winds-Of-Change/28-12-2016-110410/ (Accessed 19 June 2018).

Vance, Charles C. 1974, 1 September. *Manager Today, Executive Tomorrow*, 1st ed. New York: McGraw-Hill.

Wagner, Stephen, and Lee Dittmar. 2006, April. 'The Unexpected Benefits of Sarbanes-Oxley'. Available at: https://hbr.org/2006/04/the-unexpected-benefits-of-sarbanes-oxley (Accessed 25 June 2018).

Ward, J.L. 1991. *Creating Effective Boards for Private Enterprises: Meeting the Challenges of Continuity and Competition*. San Francisco, CA: Jossey Bass.

Wilson, O. Edward. 2012. *The Social Conquest of Earth*. New York: Liveright.

ABOUT THE AUTHORS

Walter Vieira (certified management consultant or CMC) was among the first to be elected a Fellow of the Institute of Management Consultants of India (FIMC); and also the first to start a marketing consulting company—MAS—in 1975, in Mumbai, India, after a 14-year successful career in the pharmaceutical industry, with Glaxo, Warner and Boots.

In a span of over 40 years, Walter has worked with many of the largest companies in India—both multinationals and Indian—which have been family-managed or corporates. MAS offers consulting in marketing strategy, and selection and training of marketing personnel in India, Africa, Southeast Asia and the Middle East.

Walter has published 14 books, three of them in collaboration with C. Northcote Parkinson of Parkinson Law fame. *The 5Gs of Family Business* is his sixth book published by SAGE.

He has been a business journalist, having written a fortnightly column for *Business World* for 20 years, and for *the Times of India* for 10 years; has published over 900 articles in the business and general press. He was on the advisory board of the *Journal for Management Consultants*, USA.

He is the only consultant invited to address three consecutive World Management Consultants meets in Rome, Yokohama and Berlin, and the World Marketing Summits in Dhaka and Tokyo.

He has been president of the Institute of Management Consultants of India, founder-chairman of Asia Pacific Conference of Management Consultants, and later elected chairman of the International Council of Management Consulting Institutes, the world apex body.

Walter is listed by Speakers Academy of Europe for speaking engagements worldwide. He has been a visiting professor at the Bajaj Institute of Management, Bombay University for 20 years, and he has lectured in the USA at Kellogg, Lake Forest, Rady, Drexel and Cornell, and also in Bangkok, Colombo, Singapore, Spain and Beijing.

Walter now spends considerable time in NGO work and is chairman of the Consumer Education and Research Society; trustee of MoneyLife Foundation, IDOBRO; and has been advisor to WWF for Nature for many years.

Walter is also the recipient of the Lifetime Achievement Award (LAA) for Consulting by IMC India in 2005, and another LAA for Marketing by Indys India in 2009.

Dr Mita Dixit is the co-founder of Equations Advisors Pvt Ltd. She is an advisor, researcher and educator, specialized in guiding single- and multi-generational family-owned businesses.

Mita has over 24 years of experience in family business advisory and in management consulting, strategic marketing and organizational development. She facilitates owner-families to develop a unified vision, inculcate good governance, prepare for generational transitions and lead their organizations to the next level.

At Equations, Mita provides strategic direction to the team of consultants and associates. She leads the Knowledge Forum initiative and conducts customized workshops for owner-families to enhance their capabilities, skills and performance. She mentors next-gen scions for future leadership.

Having worked in her family's business, Mita has an insider's perspective on family dynamics. She has guided several owner-families to develop and implement family constitutions and build effective board practices.

Mita has worked in corporates at senior positions in marketing and brand management. She has also worked in the academic field as the Head of Research and Consultancy for the Centre for Family Managed Business at SPJIMR, a leading B-school in Mumbai. She is a visiting faculty at renowned management institutes offering family business programmes.

A certified management consultant (CMC), a corporate director and a certified psychometric assessor, Mita is a chemical engineer with a master's in marketing management. She is the first Indian to do a doctoral research in 'Conflict and Splits in Indian Family Businesses' from BITS Pilani University.

Mita is a member of Family Enterprise Research Consortium and a member of the editorial board of the *Journal of Amity Business School*, India. Her family business case studies have won international prizes and are taught in family business courses abroad. Her research papers and articles are published in peer-reviewed journals and business magazines.

Mita speaks at national and international conferences and seminars on family-business-related topics. The media often takes her views on contemporary issues in family businesses.

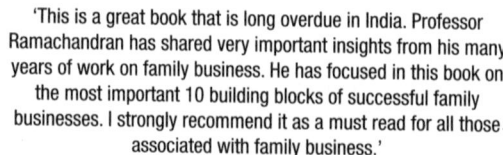
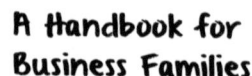

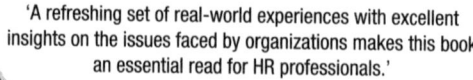